PRAISE FOR
BLACK QUEER IDENTITY MATRIX

"Sheena C. Howard offers an alternative route to studying the LGBTQI community of color. The framework outlined in this volume views gender, race, and sexual orientation as interlocking systems of oppression. This view can move us towards answering pivotal questions around gender expression, gender identity, and in-group communication patterns. I look forward to seeing the heurism of the Black Queer Identity Matrix framework."
—Cheryl Nicholas, Ph.D., Penn State University Berks

"Howard has created an important tool for methodologists, researchers, and students interested in queer studies, queer politics, and gender studies. This well-written and innovative volume provides coverage of a number of important issues for Black women of color and implications for the queer of color community as a whole."
—Rahul Mitra, Ph.D., Wayne State University

BLACK QUEER IDENTITY MATRIX

LGBT STUDIES

Judy Alston, *Series Editor*

Rochelle Brock and Richard Greggory Johnson III
Executive Editors

Vol. 56

The Black Studies and Critical Thinking series
is part of the Peter Lang Education list.
Every volume is peer reviewed and meets
the highest quality standards for content and production.

PETER LANG
New York • Washington, D.C./Baltimore • Bern
Frankfurt • Berlin • Brussels • Vienna • Oxford

SHEENA C. HOWARD

BLACK QUEER IDENTITY MATRIX
TOWARDS AN INTEGRATED QUEER OF COLOR FRAMEWORK

PETER LANG
New York • Washington, D.C./Baltimore • Bern
Frankfurt • Berlin • Brussels • Vienna • Oxford

Library of Congress Cataloging-in-Publication Data
Howard, Sheena C.
Black queer identity matrix: towards an integrated queer
of color framework / Sheena C. Howard.
pages cm — (Black studies and critical thinking; vol. 56)
Includes bibliographical references and index.
1. African American lesbians—Identity.
2. Race awareness. 3. Queer theory. I. Title.
HQ75.6.U5H69   306.76'63—dc23   2013024983
ISBN 978-1-4331-2233-0 (hardcover)
ISBN 978-1-4331-2232-3 (paperback)
ISBN 978-1-4539-1189-1 (e-book)
ISSN 1947-5985

Bibliographic information published by **Die Deutsche Nationalbibliothek**.
Die Deutsche Nationalbibliothek lists this publication in the "Deutsche
Nationalbibliografie"; detailed bibliographic data is available
on the Internet at http://dnb.d-nb.de/.

The paper in this book meets the guidelines for permanence and durability
of the Committee on Production Guidelines for Book Longevity
of the Council of Library Resources.

© 2014 Peter Lang Publishing, Inc., New York
29 Broadway, 18th floor, New York, NY 10006
www.peterlang.com

All rights reserved.
Reprint or reproduction, even partially, in all forms such as microfilm,
xerography, microfiche, microcard, and offset strictly prohibited.

Printed in the United States of America

Table of Contents

Preface vii
Acknowledgments xi
Introduction xiii

Chapter 1: Intersectionality of Black Lesbian Female Identity 1
Chapter 2: Towards an Integrated Queer of Color Framework 15
Chapter 3: The Emergence of the Black Queer Identity Matrix 39
Chapter 4: Black Queer Identity Matrix: Theoretical Framework 65

Epilogue 95
Index 103

Preface

Queer has been used as a term to describe homosexual men since the early part of the twentieth century ("Queer"); however, in the mid-to-late-1980s the term began to be redeployed as part of a utopian political project that sought to constitute and position a fluid, sexual subjectivity outside of the "heteronormative" discourses of masculine/feminine gender and homo/heterosexuality.
—Halferty, 2006, p. 125

I'm more inclined to use the words "black lesbian" because, when I hear the word queer I think of white, gay men.
—Isling Mack-Nataf (quoted in C. Smyth, 1996, p. 280)

I have to work hard to be queer. And even then, I do not think I make it. I am pretty comfortable being a lesbian. I mean, I think I get lesbianism, lesbian identity; I do not think queer is as easy to get.
—Whitlock, 2010, p. 81

I have long struggled with the term "queer." The term has a long evolving history. Although queer studies has the potential to transform the way scholars theorize sexuality in conjunction with other identity formations, the paucity of attention given to race and class in queer studies represents a significant theoretical gap (Johnson, 2001). I went back and forth several times on the title of this volume because of the use of the term "queer" and its lack of inclusion of people of color from its inception.

First, queer is used in this volume to identify anyone on the spectrum of sexual orientation outside of heterosexuality. Second, this book focuses specifically on the Black lesbian community; however, the use of the term "queer" in the title is to indicate that the work done in this book can and should be expanded upon to include any community within the queer community. Thus, it is my hope that from here, specifically racial minorities on the queer spectrum, use this as a vehicle to studying, exploring, and analyzing their own communities through an intersectional lens or through a queer matrix lens.

When I was little, around the age of six or seven, I remember the word "queer" being used to describe anyone who did not conform to heterosexuality; however, it was used in such a derogatory and insulting way. I feared to ever be called a "queer"—it sounded like one of the worse things to be called. When I first learned of queer theory during my graduate studies at Howard University, I immediately cringed at the use of the word. It was so embedded in my cultural memory as a term loaded with negative connotations. It became clear to me that scholars and activists had attempted to reclaim the term and use it as an inclusive word to describe nonheterosexual communities under one umbrella. Upon accepting the idea of "queer" as an inclusive term to describe sexual minorities, I again took issue—and still take issue—with the lack of racial inclusion within the body of literature around queer theory. It became evident to me that queer theory emerged from a Eurocentric platform in which the LGBTQ of color community was not taken into consideration, similar to the feminist movement, in which Black women felt (and were) excluded. It is because of this that I have struggled with embracing the term "queer" and using it as a catalyst or starting point in this volume. Ultimately, I have come to believe that queer theory has indeed led to the emergence of this volume, for without my disappointment in the queer theory paradigm, I would not be compelled to move scholarship or discussion toward a more integrated theoretical or conceptual framework. I view the work in this volume and the ultimate emergence of the *Black Queer Identity Matrix* as a voice within queer theorizing that offers a means of resistant expression within a given social and cultural context.

The Black Queer Identity Matrix represents research and theory that includes the experiences and ideas shared by ordinary Black, lesbian women who provide a unique angle of vision on self, community, and society. Black lesbian women are positioned within structures of power in fundamentally different ways than White queer men and women. Black lesbian organizations have faced and continue to face pushback from both the White gay community and the White lesbian community across the country. The gay rights movement is not only for gay white men. This seems to be self-evident; however, so often the visibility of the Black lesbian community is limited especially as it relates to representation within the media and politics. Thus, I would like to see a Black LGBTQ framework that re-centers the African American standpoint—that is, the historical, social and cultural underpinnings of the African American experience—as the starting place for theory and discussion through a more inductive social scientific approach as opposed to creating a theory that stems from a Eurocentric platform.

I realize that this book posits a theoretical framework that deals specifically with a minority group and the common (or not so common) experience of said group, and with that comes the immediate criticism of "essentialism" or "anti-intellectualism" from scholars. I write this book in preparation of that criticism, knowing that the fear of that criticism is much less important than the significance of this work. For any work focusing on the collective of a minority group faces the critique of essentialism.

References

Halferty, J. (2006). Queer and Now: The Queer Signifier at Buddies in Bad Times Theatre. *Theatre Research in Canada, 27*(1/2), 123–154.

Smyth, C. (1996).What Is This Thing Called Queer? In D. Morton (Ed.), *Material Queer: A LesBiGay Cultural Studies Reader* (pp. 277–285). Boulder, CO: Westview.

Whitlock, R. (2010). Getting Queer: Teacher Education, Gender Studies, and the Cross-Disciplinary Quest for Queer Pedagogies. *Issues in Teacher Education, 19*(2), 81–104.

Acknowledgments

The voices of Black lesbian women are heard throughout several pages of this book. They are women from various social locations and they are telling their stories in their own words. I wish to pay tribute to the women whose lives, one way or another, have contributed to the emergence of the conceptual framework, Black Queer Identity Matrix. The list includes those who have participated in studies within this volume or by other social scientists, as well as those who have written about their own lives or assisted me directly in writing this book. The honesty and sincerity of those who have participated in numerous studies conducted around Black, lesbian identity provided essential insights in the process of defining the Black Queer Identity Matrix and its meaning for Black, lesbian women. I pay tribute to all the friends and family who have listened and challenged my ideas over the last two years—those who have agreed with me and disagreed with me—those people have largely shaped the construction of this work.

Additionally, I wish to express my appreciation to Rider University for funding my research on the book with a Summer Research Fellowship Award. My sincerest gratitude goes out to Nikole Dorsett, my research assistant. Your hard work and dedication to this project has truly been a blessing. Finally, I would like to thank, from the bottom of my heart, all those who believed and who continue to believe in me and my work.

Introduction

Rights have always been a luxury in this country, afforded to those who are born the *proper* race, gender, and sexual orientation. Protection under the law is merely an amenity, for those who can afford it. The currency is our identity, which none of us have control over. It is this history, United States history, which gives birth to a book such as the one you hold in your hands.

If I said, "Black lesbian female" what are the first images that come to mind? What do you see? What do you associate with "Black lesbian women"? I put it in quotes because the image, if any that comes to mind, is most likely far from the image of what a Black, lesbian female looks, acts, or thinks like. Now, yes, Black lesbian women are multifarious and no two women think or act exactly alike; however, there are common struggles, experiences, and perceptions that make the Black lesbian female experience unique. The problem is, we have no vehicle to learning or experiencing the struggles and experiences of Black, lesbian women, unless we live as Black, lesbian women. This volume introduces you to the Black lesbian female and it proposes a vehicle to learning more about this community—this small, yet important niche in society. This volume begins with my journey and ends with the journey of "others" like me.

The majority of my college years, including undergraduate and graduate studies, were consumed with finding my true self—who am I? I am sure this is typical of most young adults in their early twenties. Figuring out where one belongs, where one fits in, what groups one identifies with; all things typical of a college-aged student navigating identity and self. There was, however, a struggle that set me apart from most but that also tied me together with others. It was that of my sexuality. Understanding my emotional and sexual attraction to the same sex was all very confusing. For years, I wondered why God chose to instill these feelings within me. I questioned God. I asked time and time again that these feelings be taken away. I went to bed several nights crying myself to sleep, praying that I would wake up a heterosexual. It never happened.

When I finally came to accept that I was a lesbian—after years of denial and trying to wash myself clean of any same-sex attraction or feelings I had—I fully embraced my sexual orientation. I had no choice. This was who I was. It would not go away. I would like to take a moment to emphasize, *I had no choice*. I did choose to embrace what was natural to me—attraction to women—but I did not have a choice in being attracted to the same sex.

With this newfound acceptance of my identity my world expanded. I learned that my life wasn't over because I was a lesbian; I learned that it was okay to be a lesbian and I also learned that it wasn't going to be easy.

Through my sexual identity struggle (a struggle that continues today, though not for the same reasons as my college years), I remember several instances in which I was silenced or in which I silenced myself. For the majority of my graduate studies I was afraid to speak out against heterosexism and spent a lot of time passing as "straight." I remember all those times in which I wanted to "come out" but couldn't. I remember the fear and shame in it all. This book reflects my struggles and the struggles of so many others like me. Not just those who are Black lesbian women but anyone who has been pushed to the margins, made to feel like a pariah for any reason, can relate.

Now, as an out, Black lesbian female, this book is an effort to help myself, and those like me, replace the external definitions of one's life, which have been forwarded by the dominant group, with a more authentic, self-defined standpoint.

As I have grown as a researcher (being introduced to Audre Lorde, Barbara Smith, and Patricia Hill Collins, among others) and as a person, I now know that my experiences with my sexual orientation, coupled with my race and gender, are far from unique. I am one of many, who have been similarly silenced and share in my continuous struggle.

I felt it was important to make this book academically rigorous as well as accessible to everyday people—those who are not PhDs. For if I only speak to the elite, how will my work make an impact? This volume speaks to everyone and for everyone—no matter race, class, gender, and so forth. It speaks to anyone who has struggled in some way. Thus, I hope that those who are not Black, lesbian women can read with an open mind and open heart the experiences and struggles of Black, lesbian women. I hope you, the reader, can come to understand that it is not our differences that divide us. It is our inability to recognize, accept, and celebrate those differences (See Lorde, 1986, *Poem*) The continuity of this discussion of difference, acceptance, and understanding continues here, with fresh, new insights. Thus, the purpose of this volume is to launch the first full discussion of the need for a queer of color conceptual framework around Black, lesbian female identity. Specifically, this volume addresses the necessity for a more integrated framework within queer studies, in which the variables of race-ethnicity are taken into consideration. To that end, this volume does three things: (1) it lays out a systematic conceptual framework around Black lesbian female identity that has never been done before; (2) it discusses the need for such framework within communication scholarship; and (3) it outlines the current literature around Black lesbian women, thus engaging the reader in *what we know* about the Black lesbian female identity.

We are in desperate need of paradigmatic inquiry around the intersections of gender, sexual orientation, and race-ethnicity. Current literature around queer studies does not adequately acknowledge the complexities of racial-ethnic identity coupled with gender in negotiating identity. Rather than an attempt to theorize the spectrum of racial minorities that also identify as lesbian, gay, transgender, or questioning (LGBTQ) and hence speak for and about experiences that I am not fully familiar, this volume restricts theorizing to Black lesbian women, utilizing autoethnographic as well as ethnographic approaches with the expectation that this work may be heuristically adequate in expanding across the broad range of Black queer identities and other racial minorities within the LGBTQ community.

This volume is unique in that it highlights a triple jeopardy minority group that has been historically marginalized, and it concludes with the proposal of a much-needed framework for researchers to begin to create a baseline of knowledge and research under the umbrella of the Black Queer Identity Matrix. The Black Queer Identity Matrix will allow researchers to begin to explore questions around the Black, lesbian female community such as but not limited to:

- What communication strategies do Black, lesbian females use to negotiate their sexual identity in public discourse?
- What does it mean to be a Black lesbian female in the United States?
- How is this identity distinctive?
- What structures or processes influence how Black, lesbian women look at the world? And themselves?
- What kinds of things do Black, lesbian women feel they have to give up in order to survive? How does that rearrange their worldview?

As the reader, it is important to keep in mind that this book is birthed by a communication scholar who has worked primarily in the areas of intercultural and rhetorical communication. Therefore, I do not assume to have an extensive knowledge base outside of communication studies, although throughout this volume I pull from work across various disciplines, including but not limited to psychology and sociology.

This volume is broken down into four chapters. Chapter 1, "Intersectionality of Black Lesbian Female Identity," examines what we as academicians, consumers, and researchers know about Black, lesbian, female identity and the current state of research around this community, specifically focusing on intersectionality. Chapter 2, "Towards an Integrated Queer of Color Framework," briefly surveys the conceptual frameworks within current queer studies literature and systematically addresses the rationale for the necessity of a more integrated queer of color framework. Chapter 3, "The Emergence of the Black Queer Identity Matrix," covers the empirical research employed by the author of this text, which led to the Black Queer Identity Matrix. This chapter goes into depth on the subject of the inception, results, and implications of previous research conducted by the author around the Black Queer Identity Matrix. Finally, Chapter 4, "Black Queer Identity Matrix: Theoretical Framework," outlines integral assumptions to consider, the heurism of this framework, and the ways in which researchers can employ this new tool.

Only a framework viewing gender, race, and sexual orientation as interlocking systems of oppression can move us toward answering pivotal questions around experience, identity, hegemony, and so on. Thus, the book that you hold in your hands is innovative and essential due to the emerging political and social consciousness around the LGBTQ community, as well as the emerging focus within American culture on the LGBTQ of color community.

You may ask, what is a matrix? According to Merriam-Webster's dictionary, a matrix or matrices is material in which something is enclosed or embedded, thus, something that lies within something. Black lesbian women, and any other identity within the United States, is embedded or enclosed within the fabric of the United States. The economic, political, and social structure of a system in which one is birthed plays a dominant role in shaping one's understanding of self. Our environment has the ability to shape our self-concept, influence our self-awareness, and affect our self-esteem, which creates very unique and distinctive communication patterns for individuals. This volume moves us toward understanding the collective struggles, experiences, and communication strategies particular to the Black, lesbian community through an inductive approach, beginning with existing theoretical frameworks, hypothesizing that there are patterns across the Black, lesbian community that can and should be explored or explicated and then observing these instances for commonality (or lack of commonality). The inductive approach is about creating meaning and acknowledging subjectivity—ultimately leading to critical and needed discussion, which this book wholeheartedly welcomes.

Bibliography

Lorde, A. (1986). *Our dead behind us: Poems.* New York: W.W. Norton & Company.

CHAPTER 1

Intersectionality of Black Lesbian Female Identity

There is still a paucity of research that looks at the intersections of race, gender, and sexual orientation, specifically focusing on the Black lesbian community. There is a plethora of scholarship that examines lesbian and gay representations in the media as well as the developmental process of coming out. However, a scarcity of attention has been given to Black lesbian identity, especially in the areas of the coming-out process as well as coping mechanisms developed by the community in negotiating coming out in public discourse. One of the major reasons for this void in the literature is largely due to the lack of a queer of color theoretical framework that gives researchers the tool to examining the complexity of the Black lesbian community. Therefore, there is still a gap to be filled within queer scholarship, and specifically Black queer scholarship that takes race/ethnicity into consideration when examining the ways in which Black lesbians navigate within an oppressive society.

The goal of this chapter is twofold: (1) to draw on theoretical and conceptual frameworks within current literature, especially those that position us to move toward a more integrated queer of color framework, such as intersectionality (Audre Lorde and Lisa Bowleg) and matrix of domination (Patricia Hill Collins); and (2) to illuminate the intricacies of the Black lesbian community through making connections among race, gender, and sexual orientation, specifically as it relates to intersectionality. Throughout this chapter, the examination of each of the above-mentioned frameworks will also identify where and how Black lesbian women fit into the discussion and the implications of these frameworks.

As previously mentioned, one such framework integral to the comprehension of this volume, and ultimately the Black Queer Identity Matrix, is intersectionality. Intersectionality allows us to begin to understand the intersection between historically oppressed identities all lodged on to one cultural body, such as triple jeopardy minorities—the Black lesbian female.

In recent decades intersectionality theory has become an important paradigm shift in bridging the fields of the study of race, gender, class, and sexuality (Alimahomed, 2010).Though not called intersectionality, the foundation for the theoretical consideration of race, gender, sexuality, and class was cemented by Audre Lorde through the 1960s to the 1990s. Lorde long addressed her coming-of-age story as a woman who loved women (*Zami, A New Spelling of My Name*, 1982) and the significance of difference through various essays, poems, and speeches. In *A Burst of Light: Essays* (1988), she states:

> When I say I am a Black feminist, I mean I recognize that my power as well as my primary oppressions come as a result of my Blackness as well as my womaness, and therefore my struggles on both these fronts are inseparable. (p. 20)

Lorde's ideas and struggles speak to the notion of the ways in which her multiple intersecting identities present new and distinct challenges. She continues in *A Burst of Light*:

> When I drove through the Mississippi delta to Jackson in 1968 with a group of Black students from Tougaloo, another car full of redneck kids trying to bump us off the road all the way back into town, I was a Black Lesbian. (1988, p. 23)

Prior to the theoretical contribution of intersectionality, the scholarly cannons of race, gender, class, and sexuality were once presumed to be separate and distinct from one another, and little theoretical consideration was given to the ways these systems of power overlapped (Ferguson, 2007). This resulted in the exclusion of women of color in the production of scholarship as well as social movements. Feminist women of color began to theorize their own multiple intersecting identities as both a form of resistance and as a new epistemological framework (see Alimahomed, 2010; Combahee River Collective, 1979 [1977]; Crenshaw, 1989; hooks, 1981). Women of color who were involved in the progressive movements of the 1960s and 1970s (e.g., the feminist movement and the civil rights movement) point to the ways they experienced multiple oppressions simultaneously, contrary to the experiences of White women and men of color, for whom race or gender was often their primary and only concern (Hull, Scott, & Smith, 1982). Within the field of sociology and psychology, intersectionality is theorized as interlocking systems of oppression and privilege (Collins, 1990; Bowleg, 2008). Dimensions such as age, race, gender, religion, and others are all important factors in shaping privilege and oppression among members in society; therefore, intersectionality can be used as a methodological tool to locate the particular nexus in which various axes of inequality intersect (Alimahomed, 2010).

Researchers have begun to explore some of the methodological challenges of qualitative and quantitative research that act as a dilemma for intersectionality scholarship. For example, Lisa Bowleg (2008) states:

> A key dilemma for intersectionality researchers is that the additive (e.g., Black+Lesbian+Woman) versus intersectional (e.g., Black Lesbian Woman) assumption inherent in measurement and qualitative and quantitative data analyses contradicts the central tenet of intersectionality: social identities and inequality are interdependent for groups such as Black lesbians, not mutually exclusive. In light of this, interpretation becomes one of the most substantial tools in the intersectionality researcher's methodological toolbox. (p. 312)

Thus, in chapter 3, "The Emergence of the Black Queer Identity Matrix," I consider this methodological dilemma in examining the Black lesbian identity by ethnographically probing into what it means to be a Black lesbian female in the United States through photo feedback analysis. My intersectional approach allows the participants to describe their experiences, in their own way, using photographs; thus, as the researcher I do not impose on them to rank their identities in anyway.

I began this book by focusing on intersectionality research in order to provide some clarity and understanding as to how multiple oppressed identities yield unique challenges, perspectives, and experiences for any individual, but particularly Black, lesbian women. Also, intersectionality, as a conceptual framework, provides the foundation toward a more integrated queer of color theoretical framework in which one has to understand the significance of one's identity as they work together as interlocking systems. The Matrix of Domination also provides us with a framework for understanding intersectionality with emphasis on class. Class is one of those variables that is often not adequately addressed—or even understood—as it relates to social and economic oppression; within the Black lesbian community class plays a major role in quality of life, worldview, access, and perspective.

Matrix of Domination

Viewing the world through the simultaneity of race, gender, and sexual orientation oppression and needing a conceptual lens that views Black lesbian women as having vital knowledge about their own experiences posits a humanist vision that creates new possibilities for the empowerment of the Black lesbian community. Revealing new ways of knowing allows subordinate groups to define their own reality and has far greater implications (Collins, 1990). The Black Queer Identity Matrix, explicated in chapter 4, seeks to allow us to discover how these systems of oppression interconnect as opposed to conducting research that considers race or gender or sexual orientation.

In Black feminist thought, Patricia Hill Collins reconceptualizes race, class, and gender as interlocking systems of oppression. This paradigmatic shift offered by Collins explores domination and resistance known as the Matrix of Domination. Collins (1990), in *Black Feminist Thought*, states:

> Viewing relations of domination for Black women for any given sociohistorical context as being structured via a system of interlocking race, class and gender oppression expands the focus of analysis from merely describing the similarities and differences distinguishing these systems of oppression and focuses greater attention on how they interconnect. (p. 222)

Though the Matrix of Domination particularly focuses on race, gender, and class, the Black Queer Identity Matrix, in chapter 4 of this volume, seeks to focus and expand to include an explicit emphasis on race, gender, and sexual orientation. Therefore, Black lesbian women are the center of analysis within the framework of the Black Queer Identity Matrix, which will allow researchers to also address issues of class as well as other identity variables, such as age, parental status, able-bodied, and so forth. Thus, such a framework will not only reveal vital information about the Black lesbian experience but also question Eurocentric and masculinist perspectives and approaches to research, inquiry, and analysis (see Collins, 1990). The Black Queer Identity Matrix is built on the assumption of identities as interlocking systems of oppression; this assumption is the only way we can move forward in gaining vital knowledge about the lived experiences of Black lesbian women. According to Collins, replacing additive models of oppression with interlocking ones creates possibilities for new paradigms (p. 225). The Black Queer Identity Matrix builds on the new possibilities that bell hooks (1989) and Patricia Hill Collins speak of. hooks labels this matrix a "politic of domination" and describes how it operates along interlocking axes of race, class, and gender oppression (Collins). This politic of domination refers to the ideological ground that [Black women] share, which is a belief in domination, and a belief in the notions of superior and inferior, which are components of all of those systems (hooks, 1989). This notion can be readily seen in chapter 3 of this volume as several of the participants speak of feeling inferior in many ways.

The Matrix of Domination: Politics of Representation, Race, and Class

Most of us understand a great deal about individual oppression. Often our thinking about the intersections of gender, race, and class is more additive than interlocking; we assume that with the addition of each form of difference, oppression is worsened (Champeau & Shaw, 2003). We do not realize that each oppression actually gives shape to the others and that the intersection of gender, race, and class is itself what structures each person's relationships of domination and subordination (Champeau & Shaw, 2003). Patricia Hill Collins calls this "a matrix of domination" (See Collins, 1990). Champeau and Shaw (2003) suggest

> when the barriers of gender, race, and class (as well as ethnicity, sexual orientation, age, ability, and religion) intersect in women's lives, they establish and organize social relations of domination in which each oppressive system depends on and shapes all others. (p. 208)

Social location and identity give shape to various women's experiences within the matrix of domination. Thus, the matrix of domination situates people in relation to power. For example, Black lesbianism is devalued and marginalized within the culture and economic structure of the United States—class cannot be ignored as we examine the multiple intersecting identities of the Black lesbian community as class is directly related to access to healthcare. I agree with Cornel West (1993), in his book *Race Matters*, when he states:

> The case of black women is quite different, partly because the dynamics of white and black patriarchy affect them differently and partly because the degradation of black female heterosexuality in America makes black female lesbian sexuality a less frightful jump to make. This does not mean that black lesbians suffer less than black gays—in fact they suffer more, principally owing to their lower economic status. (p. 129)

The various ways in which ideology, patriarchy, and economic status affect Black lesbian women is multilayered. Some of these intersections will be explored throughout this chapter. For example, Black lesbian women are disproportionately infected with HIV/AIDS, and this is directly related to social class, not individual choices. West goes on to state:

> This does not mean that the subculture of black lesbians is fluid and the boundaries are less policed precisely because black female sexuality in general is more devalued, hence more marginal in white and black America. (p. 129)

This notion that West speaks of—that of Black female sexuality being more devalued and marginal in White and Black America—is fairly obvious when we turn to media representations. For example, in the last decade there has been an increase in visibility for the LGBTQ community within mainstream media.

> In 1997, the now mainstream Ellen DeGeneres attracted media attention. Not only did Ellen DeGeneres come out, but the character she played on her television show, Ellen Morgan, came out simultaneously. A gay or lesbian character had not been previously depicted as a lead character on a show and portrayed by a lesbian actor. More recently, *Will & Grace* and the designers of *Queer Eye for the Straight Guy* contribute to today's gay-positive depictions in entertainment. (Howard & Lewis, 2012).

With this increased visibility for the LGBTQ community in mainstream media, young Black lesbians have almost no visible representation in mainstream media, even though the worlds they live in, the communities they are a part of, and their experiences deserve to be publicly and academically validated (Howard & Lewis, 2012). For example, in the study *African American Lesbians Watching* The L Word: *Audience Research* (Howard & Lewis, 2012), the researchers found that many Black, lesbian women find that having their identity validated in public discourse, such as the media, gives them a sense of transcendence, meaning they feel as though they are not alone. An excerpt from one of the participants in the study follows:

> Robin stated, "You learn that you are not the only person going through that situation that you're going through." However, responses that illuminated participants' identification with the show and its characters went beyond personal connections, and demonstrated a sense of *The L Word*'s role within a larger context. For example, Mary said, "The girl in Alabama who can actually come outside and be like 'yo, I'm not ashamed of who I am; I see this on TV so I know someone is watching; I know someone is like this.'" (Howard & Lewis, 2012 p. 116)

Again, validation in public discourse is essential to one's self-image and sense of authentication.

The L Word, a Showtime series that ran from 2004 to 2009, has been one of the only popular television shows depicting the LGBTQ community that has made a concerted effort to include lesbians of various ethnicities. The show featured one African American lesbian character and one Latina character. I believe this lack of visibility speaks to the boundaries that Cornell West (1993) suggests confounds Black female sexuality within the dominant ideology engrained in American culture.

> The central role of the ideology of white female beauty attenuates the expected conclusion. Instead of black women being the most sought after objects of sexual pleasure—as in the case of black men—white women tend to occupy this "upgraded", that is degraded, position primarily because white beauty plays a weightier role in sexual desirability for women in racist patriarchal America. (p. 130)

Thus, White lesbians are positioned as more desirable to mainstream audiences, particularly heterosexual male consumers, than that of Black lesbians just by the ways in which visibility is policed. This, in part, explains the lack of representation of the Black female within mainstream media. In addition, male desires or even fantasies about lesbian sex or partaking in sex with two women and the over-sexualized visibility of lesbianism within mainstream media further reinforces the dominant patriarchal order and male mythology. Thus, when lesbians are represented, they are severely misrepresented. This misrepresentation is known as "symbolic annihilation."

Researchers have accused the media not only of providing negative or stereotyped images of many groups but also of providing too few images of certain groups (Klein & Shiffman, 2009). Numerous authors have commented on the fact that many groups (e.g., racial minorities, women, homosexuals) are underrepresented in the media (see Eschholz, Bufkin, & Long, 2002; Glascock & Preston-Schreck, 2004). The media's underrepresentation or near-total absence of portraying certain groups has been termed "symbolic annihilation" (Klein & Shiffman). This term was first referenced by Gaye Tuchman et al. (1978) in a book titled *Hearth and Home*. Symbolic annihilation is a phenomenon by which the mass media omit, trivialize, or condemn certain groups that are not socially valued (Klein & Shiffman). Therefore, by omitting certain minority groups, a medium symbolically sends a message to consumers about the societal value of that group.

Representation in the media (or lack thereof) is a form of power or disempowerment. One group has the power to represent another group that is powerless in having a voice in how it is depicted. This is an illustration of the matrix of domination, for the environment gives shape to one's self-concept. This matrix of domination is also evident in healthcare.

Intersectionality, the Matrix of Domination, and Healthcare

Worldwide, of the 33.6 million people living with HIV/AIDS, 14.8 million are women; but in Africa, where the epidemic is most widespread, 12-13 women are currently infected for every 10 men (Champeau & Shaw, 2003). Slightly more than half of the 2.1 million AIDS-related deaths in 1999 were women (Centers for Disease Control National Center for HIV, STD, and TB Prevention: Divisions of HIV/AIDS Prevention, 2002a. Hereafter, CDCNC). In the United States, women represent a steadily increasing proportion of people living with HIV/AIDS (Champeau & Shaw). In 1992, women were

14% of adults and adolescents living with AIDS. By 1999, they represented 20% of AIDS cases (CDCNC, 2002a), and, in the first half of 2000, women accounted for 26% of newly diagnosed cases (CDCNC, 2002d). HIV is not infecting U.S. women proportionately, however (Champeau & Shaw).

Women of color are infected at a far higher rate than White women. Specifically, African American and Latina women number less than a quarter of all U.S. women but account for 78% of U.S. women with AIDS (CDCNC, 2002a). In 2000, 63% of newly reported AIDS cases among women were African American (Champeau & Shaw, 2003). While Latinas accounted for slightly fewer cases than White women, their rate of AIDS incidence was seven times higher (CDCNC, 2002d). With these statistics, it is obvious to see the connection between race, gender, and health; these variables cannot be viewed in isolation if we are to understand the complexity of this phenomenon. Thus, in the United States, HIV/AIDS is racialized. However, Margaret Connors (1996) adds that structural factors such as social class and economic status, far more than individual decisions, explain the patterns of HIV infection among U.S. women. These statistics illuminate just how significant social status is in the transmission of HIV/AIDS. According to the Centers for Disease Control and Prevention (2012):

> The reasons why black and Latina women are more affected by HIV and AIDS than women of other racial and ethnic groups are not directly related to race or ethnicity, but rather to the circumstances that place these women and girls at greater risk of becoming infected with HIV. These circumstances may include higher rates of HIV and other sexually transmitted infections in communities of color, limited access to high-quality health care, poverty, stigma, fear, and discrimination.

Thus, this shows that the lives of individuals who have been historically oppressed are rooted in structural inequalities based on intersections such as class, gender, and race. A macro-level analysis of economic inequality from an intersectional perspective demonstrates aptly how the social hierarchies of race, sex, sexual orientation, and others are mutually constructed in the lives of individuals who have multiple oppressed identities. The aforementioned statistics on HIV/AIDS clearly demonstrates the intricacies of race and gender as factors that position women of color to be disproportionately affected by the disease. Lesbian women of color are not excluded from these statistics as lesbian women of color reflect a community of women within the larger spectrum of females.

Again, intersectionality is a theoretical framework for understanding how multiple social identities such as race, gender, sexual orientation, disability, and so forth intersect at the micro level of individual experience to reflect interlocking systems of privilege and oppression (i.e., racism, sexism, heterosexism, classism) at the macro social structural level (Bowleg, 2012).

Intersectionality is rooted in Black feminist scholarship. Although feminist legal scholar Kimberlé Crenshaw coined the term "intersectionality" to describe the exclusion of Black women from White feminist discourse, which equated women with White, and antiracist discourse, which equated Black with men, in the 1990s, the intersectionality concept is hardly new (Bowleg, 2012). For the Black lesbian community intersections of social status, race, and gender influence access to public health, including medical and mental health. These challenges add layers to navigating within an oppressive society, whether it be negotiating the coming out process in certain spaces or the influence of effective (or ineffective) health messages.

Public health is of relevance to understanding intersectionality and the ways in which race, social class, and gender influence access to adequate health care for historically marginalized individuals, which is why I spent the last few pages providing statistics around HIV/AIDS.

Lisa Bowleg (2012), in her article "The Problem with the Phrase *Women and Minorities*: Intersectionality—an Important Theoretical Framework for Public Health," addresses some of the theoretical and methodological challenges and benefits of intersectionality for public health theory, research, and policy. Examples from HIV prevention research and practice with Black individuals, who represented 52% of new HIV cases in 2009 despite representing just 13% of the U.S. population, accentuate why fashioning health policy and prevention messages exclusively from the perspective of White middle-class populations does not always equal good public health practice (Bowleg, 2012). Thus, health advertisements are often ineffective in reaching certain minority groups. Bowleg (2012) states:

> Take the case of Black men who have sex with men (MSM) who in 2009 represented 42% of new HIV cases among MSM.[18] Early in the HIV/AIDS epidemic, the Centers for Disease Control and Prevention (CDC) learned that HIV prevention messages targeted to gay and bisexual men were failing to resonate with Black and Latino MSM who did not identify as gay or bisexual. This recognition prompted a policy change of using the MSM nomenclature in HIV/AIDS surveillance activities and reports that is now well established in HIV prevention theory, research, and practice. (p. 1269)

These types of nuances need to be continuously researched and understood so that health messages are not constructed through a White middle-class lens, which fails to reach the LGBTQ of color community. The aforementioned is just one example of the importance of intersectionality in practice and research. Furthermore, there is a growing body of research that focuses on discriminatory practices within the healthcare system (McLaughlin, Hatzenbuehler, & Keyes, 2010).

Experiences of discrimination, whether based on race-ethnicity, sexual orientation, or gender, have been linked to elevations in psychological distress and symptoms of psychopathology (McLaughlin, Hatzenbuehler, & Keyes, 2010). For example, in the study *Responses to Discrimination and Psychiatric Disorders among Black, Hispanic, Female, and Lesbian, Gay, and Bisexual Individuals*, researchers found that psychiatric disorders are more prevalent among minorities who report being subjected to discrimination within the past year. Certain responses to discrimination, particularly not disclosing it, are associated with psychiatric morbidity (McLaughlin, Hatzenbuehler, & Keyes). Further findings in the same study report:

> Black respondents reported the highest levels of past-year discrimination, followed by LGB, Hispanic, and female respondents. Across groups, discrimination was associated with 12-month mood (odds ratio [ORs] = 2.1–3.1), anxiety (ORs = 1.8–3.3), and substance use (ORs = 1.6–3.5) disorders. Respondents who reported not accepting discrimination and not discussing it with others had higher odds of psychiatric disorders (ORs = 2.9–3.9) than did those who did not accept discrimination but did discuss it with others. Black respondents and women who accepted discrimination and did not talk about it with others had elevated rates of mood and anxiety disorders, respectively. (p. 1477)

There are a myriad of strategies that individuals use to cope with stigma-related stress, and more fine-grained analysis of psychological and interpersonal responses to discrimination is warranted in future investigations (McLaughlin, Hatzenbuehler, & Keyes). These types of analyses will facilitate the identification of mechanisms linking discrimination to psychopathology, which needs to be investigated through an intersectional lens. Community connectedness also plays a pivotal role in the mental and physical health of the LGBTQ community, especially for racial minorities.

Community connectedness is the idea that being involved or connected to the LGBTQ community in some way has a positive effect on the mental and physical health of individuals. Community connectedness is defined as the convergence of individuals' desires to belong to a larger collective, establish a mutually influential relationship with that collective, satisfy their individual needs and be rewarded through their collective affiliation, and construct a shared emotional connection (Frost & Meyer, 2012). In his model of minority stress processes among sexual minority individuals, Meyer (2003) points out the importance of connectedness to the LGBTQ community as a group-level coping resource. Specifically, feeling part of a community similar to one's own may allow sexual minorities to make positive social comparisons to other people like themselves, instead of making negative comparisons based on heterosexist stigma to members of the out-group (Crocker & Major, 1989; Herek & Glunt, 1995; Meyer, 2003). For these reasons, connectedness to the LGBTQ community may play an ameliorative role in the relationship between minority stress (i.e., stigmatization, prejudice, and discrimination) and mental health (Major & O'Brien, 2005; Meyer, 2003).

Community connectedness is indeed an intersectional concern as well. As social class, race, and other factors influence the feeling or involvement within the LGBTQ community. Not all sexual minority individuals feel, or have the opportunity to feel connected to the LGBTQ community (Barrett & Pollack, 2005). Thus, it is important to understand whether subgroups of sexual minorities differ from one another in terms of the degree to which they feel connected to the LGBTQ community. Community connectedness varies greatly by social status, with working-class individuals generally demonstrating less connectedness to the community than more affluent individuals (Barrett & Pollack).

This section addressed, through an intersectional approach, some of the health disparities and nuances within the LGBTQ of color community. It was my intent to demonstrate that the theoretical framework of intersectionality as well as the matrix of domination are pivotal in research and practice. Consequently, a framework that places emphasis on race/ethnicity as well as class (class and race are inextricably linked in the United States), particularly within the communication field, is needed if we are to ever develop a robust body of literature that addresses the coping mechanisms and strategies employed by minority individuals within the LGBTQ community. For example, such a framework would allow researchers to answer pivotal questions such as, but not limited to: How can health messages more effectively reach the LGBTQ of color community? Specifically, as discussed in this chapter, how can HIV/AIDS advertisements speak directly to the LGBTQ of color community? The Black Queer Identity Matrix, through this intersectional lens, allows us to examine not only how messages are communicated to the LGBTQ of color community but also how do LGBTQ of color individuals communicate their own health issues to practitioners? Where do these individuals gain access or knowledge of health information? How important is an individual's connection to the LGBTQ of color community in receiving health messages?

Bibliography

Alimahomed, S. (2010). Thinking outside the rainbow: Women of color redefining queer politics and identity. *Social Identities, 16*(2), 151–168.

Barrett, D. C., & Pollack, L. M. (2005). Whose gay community? Social class, sexual self-expression, and gay community involvement. *The Sociological Quarterly, 46*, 436-456.

Bowleg, L. (2008). When Black + Woman + Lesbian? ≠ Black Lesbian Woman: The methodological challenges of qualitative and quantitative intersectionality research. *Sex Roles, 59*(5-6), 312-325.

Bowleg, L. (2012, July). The problem with the phrase *women and minorities*: Intersectionality—an important theoretical framework for public health. *American Journal of Public Health, 102*(7), 1267-1273.

Centers for Disease Control National Center for HIV, STD, and TB Prevention: Divisions of HIV/AIDS Prevention. (2002a). *HIV among African Americans*. Retrieved March 11, 2013, from www.cdc.gov/hiv/pubs/facts/afam.htm

Centers for Disease Control National Center for HIV, STD, and TB Prevention: Divisions of HIV/AIDS Prevention. (2002b). *HIV/AIDS among Hispanics in the United States*. Retrieved March 11, 2013 from www.cdc.gov/hiv/pubs/facts/hispanic.htm

Centers for Disease Control National Center for HIV, STD, and TB Prevention: Divisions of HIV/AIDS Prevention. (2002c). *HIV/AIDS among U.S. Women: Minority and Young Women at Continuing Risk*. Retrieved March 11, 2013, from www.cdc.gov/hiv/pubs/facts/women.htm

Centers for Disease Control National Center for HIV, STD, and TB Prevention: Divisions of HIV/AIDS Prevention. (2002d). *HIV/AIDS Surveillance in Women: L264 Slide Series (through 2000)*. Retrieved March 1, 2013, from www.cdc.gov/hiv/graphics/women.htm

Centers for Disease Control and Prevention. (2012). *National Women and Girls HIV/AIDS Awareness Day*. Retrieved October 25, 2012, from www.cdc.gov/Features/WomenGirlsHIVAIDS/

Champeau, D. A., & Shaw, S. M. (2003). Teaching about interlocking oppressions: The case of HIV and women. *Feminist Teacher, 14*(3), 208-219.

Collins, P. (1990). *Black feminist thought: Knowledge, consciousness and politics of empowerment*. London: Harper Collins Academic.

Combahee River Collective. 1979[1977] . A black feminist statement . In Z. Eisenstein Capitalist patriarchy and the case for social feminism 362-372 . New York: Monthly Review Press .

Connors, M. (1996). Sex, drugs, and structural violence: Unraveling the epidemic among poor women in the United States. In P. Farmer, M. Connors, & J. Simmons (Eds.), *Women, poverty, and AIDS: Sex, drugs, and structural violence* (pp. 91-123). Monroe, ME: Common Courage.

Crenshaw, K. (1989). Demarginalizing the intersection of race and sex: A Black feminist critique of antidiscrimination doctrine, feminist theory and antiracist politics. *University of Chicago Legal Forum*, 138-167.

Crocker, J., & Major, B. (1989). Social stigma and self-esteem: The self-protective properties of stigma. *Psychological Review, 96*(4), 608-630.

Eschholz, S., Bufkin, J., & Long, J. (2002). Symbolic reality bites: Women and racial/ethnic minorities in modern film. *Sociological Spectrum, 22*(3), 299-334.

Ferguson, R. (2007). The relevance of race for the study of sexuality. In G.E. Haggerty and M. McGarry (Eds.) *A Companion to Lesbian, Gay, Bisexual, Transgender, and Queer Studies*, (pp. 109-123). Malden, MA: Blackwell Publishing.

Frost, D. M., & Meyer, I. H. (2012). Measuring community connectedness among diverse sexual minority populations. *Journal of Sex Research, 49*(1), 36–49.

Glascock, J., & Preston-Schreck, C. (2004). Gender and racial stereotypes in daily newspaper comics: A time-honored tradition? *Sex Roles, 51*(7–8), 423–431.

Halferty, J. (2006). Queer and now: The queer signifier at Buddies in Bad Times Theatre. *Theatre Research in Canada, 27*(1/2), 123–154.

Herek, G. M., & Glunt, E. K. (1995). Identity and community among gay and bisexual men in the AIDS era: Preliminary findings from the Sacramento Men's Health Study. *AIDS, Identity, and Community: The HIV Epidemic and Lesbians and Gay Men* (pp. 55–84).

Herek, G.M. & Greene, B. (Eds.), *AIDS, Identity, and Community: The HIV Epidemic and Lesbians and Gay Men*. Newbury Park, CA: Sage (1995).

hooks, b. (1981). *Ain't I a woman: Black women and feminism*. Boston: South End.

hooks, b. (1989). *Talking back: Thinking feminist, thinking black*. Boston: South End.

Howard, S. C., & Lewis, M. (2012). African American Lesbians Watching *The L Word*: Audience research. In T. Morrison (Ed.), *Sexual Minority Research in the New Millennium*. New York: Nova Science.

Hull, Gloria T., Patricia Bell Scott, and Barbara Smith (ed.). 1982. *All the Women Are White, All the Blacks Are Men, But Some of Us Are Brave*. New York: The Feminist Press at The City University of New York.

Johnson, E. (2001). "Quare" studies, or (almost) everything I know about queer studies I learned from my grandmother. *Text & Performance Quarterly, 21*(1), 1–25.

Klein, H., & Shiffman, K. S. (2009). Underrepresentation and symbolic annihilation of socially disenfranchised groups ("out groups") in animated cartoons. *The Howard Journal of Communications, 20*(1), 55–72.

Lorde, A. (1982). *Zami, a new spelling of my name*. Watertown, MA: Persephone.

Lorde, A. (1988). *A burst of light: Essays*. Ithaca, NY: Firebrand.

Major, B., & O'Brien, L. T. (2005). The social psychology of stigma. *Annual Review of Psychology, 56*, 393–421.

McLaughlin, K. A., Hatzenbuehler, M. L., Keyes, K. M. (2010). Responses to discrimination and psychiatric disorders among Black, Hispanic, female, and lesbian, gay, and bisexual individuals. *American Journal of Public Health, 100*(8), 1477–1484.

Meyer, I. H. (2003). Prejudice, social stress, and mental health in lesbian, gay, and bisexual populations: Conceptual issues and research evidence. *Psychological Bulletin, 129*, 674–697.

Tuchman, G., Daniels, A., & Benet, J. (1978). *Hearth and home: Images of women in the mass media*. New York: Oxford University Press.

West, C. (1993). *Race matters*. Boston: Beacon.

CHAPTER 2

Towards an Integrated Queer of Color Framework

This chapter will delve into queer theory, the history of the word "queer," and the limitations of queer theory as it relates to the incorporation of people of color. Queer theory does not offer a viable framework to holistically delve into inquiry around the LGBTQ community of color. Following the discussion on queer theory, this chapter provides an overview of E. Patrick Johnson's Quare Theory, which is relevant to the discussion around conceptual frameworks that take race, gender, and sexuality into consideration.

Queer Theory

The master narrative of American culture has maintained a compulsory heterosexual notion of reality. This dominating and oppressive system is supported and embedded in institutions such as education, healthcare, marriage, and jobs. Emerging from the cracks of heteronormative reality comes the unheard, silenced, and often forgotten voices and representations of social lives and reality. Decades of scholarship and theoretical development have significantly advanced this notion in academic disciplines; specifically, cultural studies and humanities programs have begun to make room for nonnormative representations, identities, and bodies. Developing from a spectrum of fields, queer theory is a multidisciplinary approach that questions the massproduction of patriarchal-heteronormative and Euro-American imperialism, which affects the ways in which societies, people, and cultures move and develop.

Queer theory is an academic platform for scholars to challenge and deconstruct the perpetuated heteronormative rules, rituals, and liminality of gender, sex, and sexuality. A queer theoretical approach moves away from the essentialist theorizing, often found in women's studies or LGBTQ studies, and, according to Cohen (1997), towards the understanding of the "possibility of change" and "instability of sexual categories and sexual subjects" (p. 439).

More recently, scholarship has sought to understand individual and communal identifications as the foundation for social-political action, which acknowledges the connection between representation, body, and politics. Marginalized people (i.e., bodies and behaviors) experience the negative political, legal, and social effects of their position. Feminist studies, critical race studies, and gay and lesbian studies often explore these involuntary realities of people who are subjected to leading social norms. The intersections of these academic tensions, I argue, is where queer theory is born.

From a historical perspective, the term "queer" has been used as a negative descriptor for sexually deviant and abnormal people and behavior. Lesbian, gay, bisexual, transgender people, to name a few, are disregarded, silenced, and isolated by and from those deemed by society as "normal." It is not enough to only use queer as shortened jargon of LGBTQ people. Instead, "queer" allows for understanding what is acceptable by defining that which is nonnormative.

In current discourse, the meaning and identity politics of queer has shifted to take on a variety of social, political, and/or sexual descriptors. "Queer" also serves to interrogate normative structures and people while opening up the queer potentiality of what non-nonnormativity holds. According to Halperin (2003), "Teresa de Lauretis coined the phrase 'queer theory' to serve as the title of a conference that she held in February of 1990 at the University of California, Santa Cruz" (p. 339). French philosophers Michel Foucault and Jacques Derrida and other theorists such as Eve Kososfky Sedgwick, Judith Butler, and Michael Warner have heavily influenced ideas of gender and sexuality and the development of queer theory.

Postmodernism has had great impacts on queer theory. Namaste (1994), suggests, "One of the most significant aspects of Foucault's research centers around the production of the homosexual" (p. 221). Within the social construction of identities "homosexuality began to speak in its own behalf, to demand that its legitimacy or 'naturality'" be acknowledged, often in the same vocabulary, using the same categories by which it was medically disqualified" (Foucault, 1980, p. 101). The medical, psychological, legal, and literary discourse of sex and sexuality and (by default) sexual inversion and perversity has been deeply buried into social normalcies.

Much of Jacques Derrida's work focuses on the powers of language as it influences our very existence and how we create meaning in our social lives. Namaste (1994) refers to Derrida's understanding of interpretation and binary oppositions: "We are always within a binary logic, and whenever we try to break out of its stranglehold, we inscribe its very basis" (p. 223). Deconstruction can be understood as the condition of interpretation, while supplementarity is the effect of this interpretation. This awareness of supplementarity is at the center of Derrida's writing and persistently drives queer theory.

Butler is interested in the interconnectedness of sex, gender, and desire; as such, gender performativity and identity formations are situated at the core of her rhetoric. Gender is not innate; rather it is learned and maintained through the social construction of role expectations and structures. Butler (1990) argues:

> Gender is performative as acts, gestures, and desire produce the effect of an internal core or substance, but produce this on the surface of the body, through the play of signifying absences that suggest, but never reveal, the organizing principle of identity as the cause. Such acts, gestures, enactments, generally construed, are performative in the sense that the essence of identity that they otherwise purport to express are fabrications manufactured and sustained through corporeal signs and other discursive means. (p.185)

In a binary lens of sense making, sexuality must be aligned with the proper, or correct, gender. With this intersection of sex, sexuality, and gender, queer theory dialogue can be applied. Queer theory allows for the deconstruction of the performativity of our sexualized and gendered beings with purpose given to destabilizing the co-constructed categorical labels and acknowledging that people have a fluid nature.

In *The Epistemology of the Closet* (1990), Sedgwick critiques popular language regarding bodies and behaviors by discussing the historical contexts of the construction of certain words. For example, using the term "gayness" or "gay" in association of same-sex desire requires the understanding of the underlying assumptions of nouns and adjectives. She argues, "Exciting meanings of the adjective 'gay' is still a powerfully assertive act, perhaps not one to be lightly routinized by grammatical adaptations" (p. 17). She believes,

> Modern Western culture has placed what it calls sexuality in a more and more distinctively privileged relation to our most prized constructs of individual identity, truth, and knowledge, it becomes truer and truer that the language of sexuality not only intersects with but transforms the other languages and relations by which we know. (p. 3).

By defining the categories of homo-heterosexuality, all other categorical identity formations are affected; this includes the limitations set forth by binary constructions such as secrecy-disclosure, majority-minority, and feminine-masculine (p. 11).

These dialectical dimensions that Sedgwick point to also include debates of local and global sexual political discourse. Warner (1993) draws from

Sedgwick's work and discusses the necessity of transnational comparative thinking. He proposes,

> Every person who comes to a queer self-understanding knows in one way or another that her stigmatization is connected with gender, the family, notions of individual freedom, the state, public speech, consumption and desire, nature and culture, maturation, reproductive politics, racial and national fantasy, class identity, truth and trust, censorship, intimate life and social display, terror and violence, health care, and deep cultural norms about the bearing of the body. (p. xiii)

The accepted heterosexist ideology is embedded into transnational social structures, causing the astonishing absence of queerness inside the classroom. The effects of queer theory allow for critiquing the oppressive master narrative while exploring the politics of sexual possibilities outside of static sexual identifications and behaviors.

Moving beyond feminist studies and gay and lesbian studies, the development of queer theory has broadened the spectrum of benefits and knowledge experienced by scholarly audiences. Halperin (2003) suggests that queer theory has created opportunity for "the entry of queer scholarship in the academy, the creation of jobs in queer studies, and the acquisition of academic respectability for queer work" (p. 340). Additionally, queer theory is not limited by any one academic field; instead the indefinite incorporation of queer theory into many disciplines and topics is vital to understanding the limits to our constructed binary ways of thinking and value in hearing all voices and experiences.

As queer theory is situated at the intersection of social concerns and various academic disciplines, opinions and interpretations regarding queer theoretical notions are up for debate. For starters, the mother of queer theory, de Lauretis, disconnected from this phrase just a few years after coining it. She believes that instead of its ability to advance critical thought, queer theory quickly became a mainstream marketing tactic used by the very institutions she was working to critique.

The limits of the language used within queer theory are also found to be unclear. For example, understanding queer as an umbrella term for LGBTQ self-identifications promotes confusion and contradictory messages when trying to understand queer theory. Annamarie Jagose (1996) suggests, "Queer does little more than function as shorthand for the unwieldy lesbian and gay, or offer itself as a new solidification of identity, by kitting out more fashionably an otherwise unreconstructed sexual essentialism." Queer theory, although developed from the more traditional gay and lesbian studies, works to deconstruct the stabilizing notion of sex and sexuality. However, this very desire for fluidity and non-essentialism by queer scholars actually provides the limited structured rhetoric that deems identifications as fictitious. If self-identification is continuously being re-created Jagose argues, "Queer theory curves endlessly toward a realization that its realization remains impossible."

Queer theory often analyzes positions of privilege, this being cited also as its own critique. Historically, queer carries a meaning as insulting and abusive toward gay people, gay communities, and gay behaviors. This notion of "gay" often limits itself to White male gay identifications. Riggs argues, "When those of us who identify as white speak out in regards to rights, and assert that we are entitled to do so, we draw upon our privilege as white people living in a society that accords us significant social status, *regardless of our sexuality*" (as cited in Morland, 2007, p. 598). In the humbling footprints of Cherríe Moraga and Gloria Anzaldúa, E. Patrick Johnson (2005) critiques queer theory as it "is often unable to accommodate the issues faced by gays and lesbians of color who come from 'raced' communities" (p. 127). It certainly seems counterproductive for White identified people to talk in circles about the intersectionality of race, class, sexuality, and others while not having the ability to effectively recognize and analyze their own privileged status.

Quare Theory

Discussions of intersectionality have long been part of the foundational terminology within feminist academics. Many scholars and activists knowingly accept and understand the importance of and the use of engaging the position where many aspects of social constructions meet and sometimes blend. However, this is a glossy assumption created and perpetuated through White privilege. The actual implementation of addressing these intersecting pieces of identifications is often overlooked and becomes problematic and unacceptable. The development of queer theory addresses sex and sexuality as a (marginalized) element of self-identifications.

In his 2005 essay, "'Quare' Studies, or (Almost) Everything I Know about Queer Studies I Learned from My Grandmother," E. Patrick Johnson offers a critique of queer theory as it erases, or ignores, the many components of identifications, while it emphasizes Whiteness as queer normativity. Johnson suggests, "Queer theory critically interrogates notions of selfhood, agency, and experience, but is often unable to accommodate the issues faced by gays and lesbians of color who come from 'raced' communities" (pp. 126-127). Quare theory is a vehicle for simultaneously addressing sexuality, race, class, and gender as identity formations. His purpose is not to challenge the level of various experiences of oppression but to acknowledge the positions of marginalized people, specifically quare people of color.

Johnson relies on his childhood experiences and memories of family, culture, and language to develop the term "quare" and as a basis for "quaring" "queer." Johnson (2005) provides a few definitions of his use of the term "quare":

> Quare (Kwār) n. 1. meaning *queer*, also, opp. of *straight*; odd or slightly off kilter from the African American vernacular for queer, sometimes homophobic in usage, but always denotes excess incapable of being contained within conventional categories of *being*; curiously equivalent to the Anglo-Irish (and sometimes "Black" Irish) variant of queer, as in Brendan Behan's famous play, *The Quare Fellow*.
>
> —*adj*. 2. a lesbian, gay, bisexual, or transgendered person of color who loves other men or women, sexually or nonsexually, and appreciates black culture and community.
>
> —*n*. 3. one who *thinks* and *feels* and *acts* (and, sometimes, "acts up"); committed to struggle against all forms of oppression—racial, sexual, gender, class, religious, etc.
>
> —*n*. 4. one for whom sexual and gender identities always already intersect with racial subjectivity.
>
> 5. quare is to queer as "reading" is to "throwing shade." (p .125)

Gloria Anzaldúa argues that "queer is used as a false unifying umbrella which all 'queers' of all races, ethnicities and classes are shored under" (as cited in Johnson, 2005, p. 127). While this queer umbrella may provide some benefits, the truth still remains that this queer essentialism erases racial and other differences (Johnson, p. 127). Sapinoso (2009) posits, "As a racial project of intersectionality, quaring focuses on the experiences of racialized queer people and in so doing offers us the means to interrogate the hegemonic whiteness of LGBTQ studies and queer theory" (p. 8).

Johnson (2005) argues queer theory fails to acknowledge consistently "the contributions of non-white and non-middle-class gays, bisexuals, lesbians, and transgendered people of color in the struggle against homophobia and oppression" (p. 130). Lee (2003) explains that quare studies "is an invention that dreams of the forgotten localities inhabited by shadowy figures—black, poor, male and female—multiply erased in the incubating but hegemonic queer hierarchies" (p. 161). Johnson addresses this act of minimizing the level of production of LGBTQ people of color by queer theorists by discussing performance and performativity.

Quare theory uses theories of performance and as such Johnson relies on Butler's discussion of gender performance for explanations. The notion of quare theory requires that identifications be historically and culturally situated. Johnson (2005) argues, "People have a need to exercise control over the production of their images so that they feel empowered" (p. 138). Turner defines performative reflexivity as the behavior of "a sociocultural group . . . reflect[ing] back upon themselves, upon the relations, actions, symbols, meanings, codes, roles, statuses, social structures, ethical and legal rules, and other sociocultural components which make up their public selves" (as cited in Johnson, p. 138).

Johnson (2005) relates his quare theory to Muñoz's dis-identification theory that "reflects the process through which people of color have always managed to survive in a white supremacist society" (p. 139). People of color must maintain a strategy to "work on and against oppressive institutional structures" (p.139) while being situated within and conditioned by these same structures. For example, RuPaul is among many "quares of color" who have (re)invented themselves by highlighting the transformation of their materialistic realities.

Quare theory respects and embraces identification politics while acknowledging the art of performance, which is continually, and will forever be, embedded in historical and cultural contexts. For this reason, implications of quare theory expand beyond academia and into public sphere. In the effort of expanding the rhetoric of queer theory to fully engage all intersecting identifications, I argue, Johnson has found and identified his own positionality within the institution and politics of privileged academia and performance. The Black Queer Identity Matrix seeks to explore that positionality for the Black lesbian female as well.

Race Relations and the LGBTQ Community

With the continual discussion of one's positionality and the ways in which non-White members of the LGBTQ community expand their experiences beyond academia, it is important to delve into race relations within the LGBTQ community. This discussion will begin with the present state of the gay rights movement and racism within and across the LGBTQ community.

It has been my experience as a member of the Black lesbian community that many gay or lesbian individuals, especially White members of the community, do not feel comfortable talking about race relations as it relates to the LGBTQ community, whether it be because some people simply do not see race relations as an issue in the community or because some people feel as though not talking about it will make it go away. However, as a Black lesbian female my positionality is that racism is a significant problem within the community, and it is my stance that nothing improves when an issue is silenced. I address this topic knowing that it will be uncomfortable for some and undoubtedly some others will not agree with my conclusions; however, the fear of rejection is not stronger than the need for change. The exploration and examination of race relations within the LGBTQ community gives rise and need to a theoretical framework that seeks to expound upon these issues. If Queer Theory does not create a space to delve into race, there needs to be a movement of conceptual frameworks that find it important and necessary.

Gay Marriage, the Gay Rights Movement, and Race

Since gay marriage equality is obviously advantageous to gay men and lesbian women of all classes and races, it would appear that even vastly dissimilar gay rights groups and organizations would unite around this issue. In reality, however, the gay marriage equality movement has seldom succeeded in uniting gay men and lesbian women of different social backgrounds, and rarely have the movement leaders popularized the genuine concerns of working-class men and women or the LGBTQ of color community. Moreover, arguments advanced by gay marriage advocates have sometimes been based on blatantly racist premises, which this chapter will touch upon. The progressive potential of gay marriage equality remains indisputable, but in actuality the historical record of this movement leaves much to be desired in the realm of challenges to racism and racist exploitation. For example, let's take a look at Proposition 8 in California.

Proposition 8, also known as the California Marriage Protection Act, was a ballot initiative approved by a majority of California voters on November 4, 2008, that modified California's constitution to prohibit same-sex marriage. Coincidentally, November 4, 2008, was the historical election of President Barack Obama, the nation's first Black president. On November 4, 2008, more than 50% of the voters agreed to eliminate the right of same-sex couples to marry in the state of California. Article I, Section 7.5 was added to the California Constitution stating that only marriage between a man and a woman is valid or recognized in California. If anyone had any doubts about racism in and across the gay rights movement, there should have been nothing to doubt after the reaction of the LGBTQ community to the passing of Prop 8. There was a full-out "blame the Blacks" smear campaign after Prop 8 was passed.

Just days after the election, *The Los Angeles Times* printed Associated Press exit poll data indicating that 70% of African American voters (compared with 53% of White voters) had supported the ban on gay marriage, provoking a firestorm of commentary about the racial divide between the gay community and communities of color (Stone & Ward, 2011).

Everyone should have seen this coming, since historically the LGBTQ of color community had and has been ignored. What can one expect if you refuse to target and direct campaigns toward the entire community and communities within the community? The gay White male has long been and continues to be the face of the movement. Gay men and lesbian women were quick to point fingers and it should seem odd that one day the gay community is walking hand in hand in the fight for gay rights and the next day (after November 4), the gay community is hurling racist comments at Blacks and blaming them for the passing of Prop 8. A blog titled, *N-Word Hurled at Blacks during Westwood Prop 8 Protest*, written on November 7, 2008, by ROD 2.0 states:

> Not that this wasn't expected. The recent passage of California's Proposition 8 has exposed some of the latent racism of many within the LGBTQ community—instigated in part by many in the e-telligentsia such as revisionist Andrew Sullivan and sex advisor turned sociologist Dan Savage. Unfortunately the "blame the blacks" meme is being commonly accepted by some so-called "progressive" gay activists. A number of Rod 2.0 and Jasmyne Cannick readers report being subjected to taunts, threats and racist abuse at last night's marriage equality rally in Los Angeles.

A story on the same blog site reported an incident in which two Black men were carrying NO ON PROP 8 signs and were subjected to abuse:

> Three older men accosted my friend and shouted, "Black people did this, I hope you people are happy!" A young lesbian couple with mohawks and Obama buttons joined the shouting and said there were "very disappointed with black people" and "how could we" after the Obama victory. This was stupid for them to single us out because we were carrying those blue NO ON PROP 8 signs! I pointed that out and then one of the older men said it didn't matter because "most black people hated gays" and he was "wrong" to think we had compassion. That was the most insulting thing I had ever heard. I guess he never thought we were gay.

There are enough of these types of stories to fill up this entire volume; this demonstrates the ugly head of racism within and across the LGBTQ community. Racism did not suddenly emerge due to the unfortunate result of Prop 8; it has always been there. I could make a claim that White Republicans, Mormons, and other groups are responsible for the outcome of Prop 8 but that would be pointing the finger in the same way in which Blacks were blamed for the outcome. At the end of the day, the outcome of Prop 8 was a collective effort in which not only Blacks were responsible, but also the disengagement of the gay rights movement with members of color divided the community and did not provide a vehicle in which people of color felt part of the movement. Outreach to the LGBTQ of color community long before Prop 8 should have been a plan of galvanizing LGBTQ people of color in the fight for equality together. Why? Because the more LGBTQ people of color are able to successfully come out of the closet and remain visible, then more acceptance will be garnered within those individuals' families and communities. When you have a family member or friend that is on the LGBTQ spectrum, you are more likely to stand on the side of LGBTQ equality and policy. When one feels a part of a community, one will be more likely to remain visible. The LGBTQ community needs to do a better job of creating that safe space for members of color.

When I turned on the news as a Black lesbian woman the day after President Obama was elected as the first Black president, I felt a sense of pride and transcendence. I also felt a sense of sadness that Prop 8 passed. When I saw the reaction of the gay community and the name calling, racial slurs, and disdain the gay community demonstrated as they pointed fingers at the entire Black community, I found myself betwixt and between. Stone and Ward (2011) state:

> Popular national television commentators from Bill O'Reilly to Jon Stewart bantered about Black voters turning out in large numbers to elect Barack Obama and "advance their own civil rights," while on the same ballot denying equal rights to lesbians and gay men. This suggestion that Black voters were hypocritically celebrating a victory for racial justice while perpetuating a newer and more socially accepted form of discrimination rapidly became a popular theme among White lesbian and gay activists in California. Fuelled by media spin and their own racism, White activists at statewide gay and lesbian protests aggressively blamed Black bystanders, tossed about racist slurs with a new sense of entitlement, declared "Gay is the new Black!" (p. 606)

Ultimately, Black lesbians and gay men were demanded to account for the homophobia of "their race" (see Stone & Ward, 2011).

The Black community is not entirely homophobic and it was and is extremely unfair for Blacks to be overwhelmingly blamed for the passing of Prop 8, but someone had to be blamed.

When queer protest shifted from Black voters to the Mormon Church (the latter had raised considerable funds in support of the ban), White Mormon leaders responded by comparing their persecution at the hands of angry lesbians and gay men to that of Black civil rights leaders in the South, in turn drawing criticism from Black communities (Stone & Ward, 2011, p. 606).

This alignment of the civil rights movement to the gay rights movement has continually been a point of contention as far as race relations are a concerned in and outside of the LGBTQ community.

The Gay Rights Movement and the Civil Rights Movement

Numerous studies of the gay rights movement in the United States have documented the ways in which its White leadership, with aspirations to White- and upper-middle-class normativity and cooptation of Black civil rights language, have constrained its progress since the 1970s. White leadership also has continually constructed gayness as White and posited gays and people of color as mutually exclusive and oppositional groups (see Stone & Ward, 2011). Both of the abovementioned work to inhibit progress as it relates to LGBTQ equality.

For many in the black community, the problem(s) with the gay rights movement attempting to align itself with the civil rights movement is that (1) Blacks feel political ownership over the civil rights movement; (2) the civil rights movement was birthed out of the Black church; and (3) sexual orientation is a choice that can be changed and skin color is not. I do not agree with all three of these reasons, but they largely fuel the contention between aligning the gay rights movement with the civil rights movement. Ultimately, I do not believe this alignment is an effective rhetorical strategy as far as increasing acceptance and support within the LGBTQ community.

There remains strong Christian ideals and values within and across the African American community. The civil rights movement emerged out of the Black church, which adds a layer of contention when one begins to align the civil rights movement with the gay rights movement. Yes, it comes down to race and the historical underpinnings of the movement and the Black community. Understanding a community's cultural history and collective is essential in understanding the worldview of a people and one of the most important assumptions of the Black Queer Identity Matrix. However, even more important is the fact that there should never be a comparison of any historically oppressed group or movement that makes the comparison of the two movements intrinsically problematic.

Minister Voddie Baucham, from the Grace Family Baptist Church in Spring, Texas, has publicly stated that "homosexuals have effectively co-opted blackness . . . to where now, we actually believe gay is the new black and we actually believe homosexual marriage is a civil rights issue." Baucham continues, "I'm insulted that people equate not just a sinful behavior but a behavior that's a special category of sin called abomination with the level of melanin in my skin" (as cited in Phan, 2011). Many Black religious leaders, including Baucham, feel as though the civil rights movement was not at all inclusive of members of the LGBTQ community and that anything outside of heterosexuality is a sin. Reverend William Owens, founder and leader of the Coalition of

African American Pastors (CAAP) in Tennessee, states, "The homosexual community has taken the Civil Rights movement and hijacked it. . . . I was in the Civil Rights Movement and I can tell you I did not march one inch, one foot, one yard, one mile for same-sex marriage" (as cited in Coleman, 2012). The Coalition of African American Pastors states in the following release:

> The hijacking of the civil rights movement by homosexuals, bisexuals and gender-confused people is unacceptable. There is no legitimate comparison between skin color and sexual behavior. In addition, the high cost of achieving racial parity by ours and previous generations demands that we speak out against President Obama's support for this destructive agenda. Our God requires it, our nation needs it and our people deserve it. ("Coalition of African American Pastors," 2012)

For these outspoken leaders, civil rights around alternative sexual orientations are illegitimate, and it is most evident that these views are largely founded in the Black church. According to the logic by these prominent voices in the Black community, being a member of the LGBTQ community is not only a sin but also a choice; therefore, there are no civil rights to be fought for the LGBTQ community since one can choose to be heterosexual. These Black religious leaders find the juxtaposition of civil rights and gay rights appalling. Leaders outside of the church and of various racial backgrounds share this same sentiment. For example, Paul M. Weyrich, from the Committee for the Survival of a Free Congress, writes:

> There should be a social stigma attached to homosexuality. The idea that homosexuality should be a protected civil right is an outrage. I have told black and Hispanic audiences that no one should be more enraged by this concept then they. What these deviants are suggesting is that somehow their immoral behavior is on a par with being black or on a par with being Hispanic. Now, if I were black or Hispanic, I would be incensed by this because there is something which is an act of God, namely, what race I was born into, being equated with a choice for deviant behaviors. (Decter, Stanton Evans, Falwell, et al., 1984, p. 24)

From my perspective, the fact is that not all blacks support gay rights and not all LGBTQ people supported black rights during the civil rights movement. Not all women supported Black rights during the woman's movement. Black queer people are beneficiaries of the civil rights movement and Black gay people realize that racism is still alive and well. It is essential that LGBTQ people of color have a safe space to be out and have support from the gay community in achieving visibility. The fact of the matter is, the more minorities come out of the closet, the more various heterosexual communities will be accepting and supportive of "gay rights" because they will know that their brothers, sisters, cousins, best friends, and nephews are on the LGBTQ spectrum. When all that is depicted in mainstream media, popular culture, and politics are White, gay men, there is no outreach to ethnic communities, thus no or very limited progress for the gay rights movement. Therefore, blanket statements that the gay rights movement is the new civil rights movement are offensive to a large majority of the Black community. Especially, as many Blacks today—LGBTQ or heterosexual—do not feel as though they are treated as equal citizens, although we are said (incorrectly) to be living in "postracial" America. If we are living in postracial America, why is the LGBTQ community so segregated?

The ranks of the gay rights movement historically did not include substantial numbers of people of color. Segregation of the gay community isn't more evident than in each major city in America having separate Gay Pride and Black Gay Pride events. Given the racial composition of the larger gay rights movement, this should not at all be surprising. The absence of racial minorities as the face(s) of the gay rights movement lay in the ideological underpinnings of the gay rights movement itself. First, the failure of the gay rights movement to conduct a historical self-evaluation led to a dangerously superficial appraisal of Black people's suspicious attitudes toward gay marriage equality and an assumption that Black people *ought* to support gay rights because they are minorities themselves. In rhetorical communication, this would be considered an invalid syllogism, in which you can clearly see an invalid deduction. Furthermore, when gay White people unhesitatingly equate the gay rights movement with the civil rights movement, it appears to be exaggerated because minorities have not been represented within the gay rights movement in the first place. The aftermath of Prop 8 was an important clue about the history and present condition of the gay rights movement and perhaps an unfortunate but much needed wake-up call. White gay rights leaders cannot invoke Blackness or, in this case, the civil rights movement, when it is politically convenient, which is what the statement, "The gay rights movement is the new civil rights movement" does. The notion that one is entitled to use racial history in this country as a means of political convenience is, indeed, a symptom of White privilege.

White Privilege and the Gay Rights Movement

Rights have always been a luxury in this country, afforded to those who are born the *proper* race, gender, and sexual orientation. Protection under the law is merely an amenity for those who can afford it. The currency is our identity, which none of us have control over. It is this history—United States history—that gives birth to a book such as the one you hold in your hands. From nineteenth-century physicians to twentieth-century religious leaders, White heterosexuals seeking to regulate both queerness and Blackness have worked not only to define these as comparable but mutually exclusive formations (Stone & Ward, 2011), but also to ensure that zero-sum gay versus Black frameworks remain at the heart of the most significant gay rights debates in the United States (Stone & Ward, 2011, p. 607). For instance, there was a gay myth used against the Gay Rights movement in the 1990s, which is the notion that gays are the wealthiest demographic group in the country. Not only is this myth problematic for the gay community at large but it is even more problematic for LGBTQ members of color, particularly, as poverty levels for Blacks and Hispanics continually exceed the national average and these numbers include gay and lesbian individuals. Thus, the notion that gay people are the wealthiest minority in the country (1) does an injustice to a complete understanding of social class as it relates to diversity of the LGBTQ community in this country, and (2) clearly does not take into account the vast majority of gay and lesbian individuals in this country as class and race are inextricably linked. The gay community in the United States is as diverse as the population at large—when will minorities be included in discussions of gay rights outside of including them when it is convenient or when a scapegoat is needed? Outside of the perceptions of social status that have been created around the LGBTQ community, the two major aims of the gay rights movement are marriage equality and open inclusion in the military. These issues, which fuel the gay rights movement, are not issues representative of the multifaceted individuals that make up the LGBTQ community. Though all members of the gay and lesbian community will benefit from marriage equality and inclusion in the military, these political agendas do not address the primary concerns of racial minorities. Thus, despite the growing visibility of queer communities of color, the mainstream gay community and its political aspirations remain White in its orientation (Teunis, 2007). These political issues at the forefront of the gay rights movement position the gay-lesbian community as monolithic or "singular." For example, many scholars (Rofes, 1998; Teunis, 2007) find it inherently problematic and a rhetorical choice to refer to the gay community as a singular community, arguing that there are multiple gay communities. Teunis states:

> Marriage equality and military service are the main political items, right now, both of which serve a mainly white gay community. These political agendas do not address the primary concerns of those within the gay community who are non-white, or poor, or young. Speaking of a single gay community is therefore a rhetorical choice, just as speaking of multiple gay communities is. There is no inherent "truth" to either position, but a political aim to highlight one feature or another. (p. 264)

I particularly agree when speaking of the rhetorical choices one uses in describing any community as they often have subtextual meanings. For example, I have seen a gradual change in the use of LGBTQ and GLBTQ to describe the spectrum of sexual orientation. I purposely use LGBTQ as opposed to GLBTQ because I believe there are ideological considerations that not even the gay-lesbian community can escape. Positioning GLBTQ is a form of patriarchy in which gay—which refers to males—is positioned before lesbian, which refers to women. This is also readily seen as often we refer to the community as "gay," which can encompass both men and women, however "lesbian" merely refers to women. This is symptomatic of the patriarchy that exists within the fabric of American culture—just as "man" used to be an all-encompassing term to include both men and women. More and more national organizations, including the National Communication Association, use the acronym GLBT. Furthermore the community has often been represented as a predominately White community (Murray, 1996) and, I would argue, as a predominately White male community, especially as it relates to the gay rights movement. Currently, the LGBTQ political rests on the unproblematic assumption of the Whiteness of its goals and constituents. According to Tenuis (2007), "Gay men and lesbians who want to serve in the military are perceived as white; gay marriage is often portrayed as the extension of white privilege to the gay community" (p. 265). Without the struggle for gay marriage, in what ways would White gay men be oppressed? Just because the lesbian-gay community is a minority community in the United States does not make it immune to the systemic and cultural oppressive ideologies that fuel American politics and ideology. Racism in the lesbian-gay community follows a cultural logic as Whiteness is a major part of the LGBTQ movement. These are all nuanced issues that need to be brought to the forefront and discussed in an open and honest space on a daily basis. These issues around race relations are the impetus of the Black Queer Identity Matrix. These concerns speak to the need for a queer of color framework. These concerns can also be found is the historicity of the women's rights movement.

Implications of the Women's Rights Movement

For the remainder of this chapter, I will switch gears to focus on the historical ramifications of race relations within and across the women's movement. As a member of the Black lesbian community and as someone who has lived and traveled to various states all over the country, I am well aware of the butch-femme dichotomy that is so prevalent and essential to dating within the Black lesbian community. Not much has been written on the intricacies of Black relationships as it specifically relates to gender presentation and the butch-femme dichotomy. Scholar Mignon R. Moore has done some very interesting and distinctive research around this area, as she connects gender presentation in the Black lesbian community to 1970s feminism.

This section serves to create continuity between the state of the Black lesbian community today and the history of the feminist movement. This will allow me to illuminate the unique challenges the Black lesbian community has faced and continues to face in the twenty-first century and beyond. Thus, the complexities of race, gender, and sexual orientation will continue to be illuminated throughout the volume.

First, as with all lesbian communities, there are various physical representations of gender in Black lesbian communities. This is not something new and distinctive within the Black community. There are numerous labels to categorize lesbians including femme, butch, stud, soft-stud, aggressive, aggressive femme, and the list goes on and on. It is true that some of these terms are more prevalent within the Black lesbian community as opposed to other lesbian communities. It is also true that these labels within the lesbian community suggest expectations for and within relationships. Mignon Moore (2006) states:

> In most cases, feminine looking women partner with women who are not as feminine in their physical style and mannerisms . . . even when women have a preference for a particular gendered display, so I do not like to acknowledge the significance of categories and their meanings for their personal preferences. (p. 114)

This butch-femme dichotomy, as I like to call it, is a general pattern within and around Black lesbian relationships; however, there are those who are feminine who ONLY prefer very feminine women as partners. Even still the trend of feminine women seeking less feminine women cannot be denied due to its overwhelming frequency within the community. Thus, the existence and meaning of gender presentation within the Black lesbian community is a phenomenon that needs to be further explored and connected to historical and cultural underpinnings. Moore (2006) suggests that Black women-identified women were not one group of lesbians who were fully indoctrinated into the particular type of feminism espoused during the 1960s and 1970s. Of course, we do have historical accounts that echo the aforementioned statement and explore how Black lesbian women felt about the women's liberation movement. For example, in the 1980s Audre Lorde and Barbara Smith were very outspoken about the racism within and across the women's movement. A paper delivered at the Copeland Colloquium at Amherst College in 1980—and included in the book *Sister Outsider*, 1984—Lorde states:

As white women ignore their built-in privilege of whiteness and define woman in terms of their own experience alone, then women of color become "other", the outsider whose experience and tradition is too "alien" to comprehend. (p. 117)

Black lesbians were not only concerned with women's rights but they also lived in a world in which racial interests were important to them as well. These racial interests were often not seen as mutual or inclusive within the feminist movement. White women have reported that Black women wanted their own issues at the forefront of the movement and wanted to blame White women for their subjugation instead of directing that anger toward men (Calderone & Charoula, 1980). It is this segregation and discontent with the feminist movement that led to the development of Black lesbian communities outside of and distanced from the feminist movement and lesbian-feminist. Black feminist movements such as womanism emerged; however, even a movement such as womanism was not largely concerned with lesbian inclusions. While the history of the African American experience has been poorly documented, we know that an extensive, private, and racially homogeneous social life has existed for Black lesbians as early as the 1920s in Harlem (Garber, 1990). Consequently, this also influenced gender presentation, gender expression, and gender oppression. According to Moore (2006), since many Black women were never fully part of White lesbian-feminist leadership or on board with all of its goals, they were less influenced by efforts to replace butch and femme identities with androgynous presentations of self (p. 117).

Womanism and Black Feminism

So far, I have spoken in general terms about the lack of inclusion Black women experienced when it came to the women's rights movement and how that ultimately influenced gender roles and gender presentation within the Black lesbian community. Therefore, time needs to be dedicated to questions such as: What movements emerged due to this lack of inclusion? Why do Black women feel the need to create a movement outside of the women's rights movement? How did Black women modify the term "feminism?" I will begin this discussion by focusing on "womanism," a term coined by Alice Walker in 1984.

Womanism emerged out of a consciousness within the Black female community around the unique experiences of women of color. In a sense, womanism emerged out of "Black feminist thought," but, the term "Black feminism" was not defined until 1990 in Patricia Hill Collins's book, *Black Feminist Thought*.

Many Black women have and continue to view feminism as a collection of movements that have historically excluded or been insensitive to the issues of their community—the intersection of race, class, and gender. Many Black women view feminism as a movement that at best is exclusive of women and at worst dedicated to attacking or eliminating men (Collins, 1990). Collins provides an overview of some of the ideological differences between Black feminism and womanism in her article titled, "What's in a Name? Womanism, Black Feminism and Beyond" (2001). My position is that the discussion of the differences between the two terms seems to serve as a distraction from the underpinnings of women's rights for the Black female community. Furthermore, many people use the terms "Black feminism" and "womanism" interchangeably because both aim to fight against sexism and racism. Therefore, it is not my purpose or intention to categorize one over the other; however, as it is my objective to provide an overview of the history of Black women as it relates to creating awareness or a level of consciousness around Black female liberty and equity, this discussion will focus on womanism and Black feminism.

"Womanism" is a term that Alice Walker coined in the volume *In Search of Our Mothers' Gardens: Womanist Prose* (1983). In it she states:

1. From *womanish*. (Opp. of "girlish," i.e., frivolous, irresponsible, not serious.) A black feminist or feminist of color. From the black folk expression of mothers to female children, "you acting womanish," i.e., like a woman. Usually referring to outrageous, audacious, courageous or *willful* behavior. Wanting to know more and in greater depth than is considered "good" for one. Interested in grown up doings. Acting grown up. Being grown up. Interchangeable with another black folk expression: "You trying to be grown." Responsible. In charge. *Serious*.
2. *Also:* A woman who loves other women, sexually and/or nonsexually. Appreciates and prefers women's culture, women's emotional flexibility (values tears as natural counterbalance of laughter), and women's strength. Sometimes loves individual men, sexually and/or nonsexually. Committed to survival and wholeness of entire people, male *and* female. Not a separatist, except periodically, for health. Traditionally a universalist, as in: "Mama, why are we brown, pink, and yellow, and our cousins are white, beige and black?" Ans. "Well, you know the colored race is just like a flower garden, with every color flower represented." Traditionally capable, as in: "Mama, I'm walking to Canada and I'm taking you and a bunch of other slaves with me." Reply: "It wouldn't be the first time."

3. Loves music. Loves dance. Loves the moon. *Loves* the Spirit. Loves love and food and roundness. Loves struggle. *Loves* the Folk. Loves herself. *Regardless.*
4. Womanist is to feminist as purple is to lavender.

Alice Walker's choice of the term "womanist" instead of "feminist" was indeed a political statement and a clear split from some of the assumptions or ideologies of feminism during the 1980s. Furthermore, womanism, as a movement, was largely in response to the women's rights movement being oblivious or insensitive to African American women's ideas, histories, and experiences. Groundbreaking works by Toni Cade, Audre Lorde, June Jordan, and many other Black women in the 1980s and 1990s provided Black women with an achieved level of visibility. Womanism's precepts bear a strong resemblance to those of the Combahee River Collective, whose 1977 statement also asserts the possibilities for liberation found in Black women's identities, voices, and political work. Womanism is rooted in racial and gendered oppression as experienced by women of African descent in America while simultaneously upholding positive relationships between men and women. In addition, womanism is one that evolves continually through its rejection of all forms of oppression and commitment to social justice (Collins, 1990). Almost from its inception in the nineteenth century, the women's movement has been viewed as the "White women's movement." Tally (1986) states:

> In the 1960's Civil Rights movement, even while the seeds of female liberation were once again being planted and nurtured, hostility between white and black women intensified: while black women and men marched shoulder to shoulder, endured beatings and insults together and were likewise equally likely to get thrown in jail, after hours black men went out with and bedded down with the newly liberated white women. (p. 207)

Here you can see the tension between White women and Black women, layered by the unity that both Black men and women shared due to racial injustice in America. It is documented that oftentimes when Black women did participate in the women's movement, they were not welcome with open arms. Tally goes on:

> While the established definition of feminism is the theory of the political, economic, and social equality of the sexes, white women liberationists used the power granted to them by virtue of their being members of the dominant race in American society to interpret feminism in such a way that it was no longer relevant to all women. And it seemed incredible to black women that they were being asked to support a movement

> whose majority participants were eager to maintain race and class hierarchies between women. (p. 207)

Several writings by Black women, such as Audre Lorde and Barbara Smith, express the same sentiment as described above. Black women were also asked to reconcile their gender and race by focusing on what at the time seemed to be the lesser of two evils—racism was much greater. So long had American society emasculated the Black man that to focus upon sexism rather than racism as the cause of their plight was seen by most women as little less than treason (Richie, 1985).

Black Feminism

According to Patricia Hill Collins (1990), using the term "Black feminism" disrupts the racism inherent in presenting feminism as a for-Whites-only ideology and political movement. Black feminism is a reminder that White women are not the cultural owners of feminist consciousness. Similar to this notion is that within the gay community there are several communities comprised of various people of color. Therefore, the concept of varying levels of consciousness from culture-centered perspectives within feminism follows the same logic.

The term "Black feminism" is often associated with American and White because the feminist movement was said to be a White, middle-class movement for women. Thus, Black women have difficulty aligning themselves with Black feminism as opposed to womanism. Womanism explicitly posits that it is for the equality of both men AND women and the strengthening of male-female dynamics in the Black community. Black feminism seeks to ensure political rights for Black women and stresses the importance of political issues within and around the Black female community. Collins (1990) states:

> The emphasis on themes such as personal identity, understanding "difference," deconstructing women's multiple selves, and the simplistic model of the political expressed through the slogan the "personal is political," that currently permeate North American white women's feminism in the academy can work to sap black feminism of its critical edge. (p. 14)

Another unfortunate challenge facing Black feminism is the association with the terms "feminism" and "lesbianism." Feminism has long been linked to lesbianism. This is especially problematic within the Black community as strong Christian values are often underpinnings within Black thought and consciousness. Though many African American women may be comfortable with gay men and lesbian women, many are not, and thus we have a distancing of Black women from Black feminism because of its acceptance of or connection to lesbianism. Collins (1990) states that one Black woman questioned, "Why do I have to accept lesbianism in order to support black feminism?" (p. 14). The answer is, you don't! However, for those unaccepting of orientations outside of heterosexuality, the fact of the matter is that within the Black female community there are a variety of communities—there are lesbian women, bisexual women, transgendered women, and so on. If one is for the rights of all women, then one should be for the rights of all women regardless of sexual orientation. That is not at all to say that Black women have to support gay rights. Therefore, the question of "having to accept lesbianism" is a moot point if you are indeed participating in a movement that is for the equality of all women. In addition, lesbianism and feminism are often associated with women that hate men. Again, though there may be lesbians that disassociate themselves with men or do not like men, from my experience that is not the majority of lesbians.

> This reduction not only constitutes a serious misreading of black lesbianism—black lesbians have fathers, brothers, and sons of their own and are embedded in a series of relationships as complex as their heterosexual brothers and sisters. (Collins, 1990, p. 14)

The discussion of the differences of Black feminism and womanism is one that needs to be reviewed as was done here; however, seeking to create a wedge between the two paradigms is counterproductive to Black women's rights. Audre Lorde's words resonate well with the sentiment that *the master's tools will never dismantle the master's house*. This discussion was merely to briefly describe the history of the Black feminist movement and to identify, in some ways, where lesbianism fits into the conversation. Furthermore, conversation around the differences between the two movements generally never leave academe, as every day Black women are concerned with equal rights, not in the defining of terms. Collins (1990) states:

> Black women academics explore intriguing issues of centers and margins and work to deconstruct black female identity while large numbers of black women remain trapped in neighborhoods organized around old centers of racial apartheid. (p. 15)

Bibliography

Butler, J. (1990). Performative acts and gender constitution: An essay in phenomenology and feminist theory. In Sue-Ellen Case (Ed.), *Performing feminisms: Feminist critical theory and theatre* (pp. 270-282). Baltimore: Johns Hopkins University Press.

Butler, J. (2006). *Gender trouble*. New York: Routledge. (Original work published 1990)

"Coalition of African American Pastors Coalesces Key Civil Rights Leaders for Marriage." (2012, May 15). Retrieved from http://www.prweb.com/releases/2012/5/prweb9499716.htm

Calderone, L. & Charoula. 1980. "The Personal Is Political Revisited: An Exploration of Racism in the Lesbian Community." In J. Gibbs & S. Bennett (Eds.), *Top Ranking: A Collection of Articles on Racism and Classism in the Lesbian Community*, (pp. 79–84). New York: February 3rd.

Cohen, C. J. (1997). Punks, bulldaggers, and welfare queens: The radical potential of queer politics? *GLQ: A Journal of Lesbian & Gay Studies*, 3(4), 437–465.

Coleman, A (2012). Black Pastors Say Gay Marriage Hijacks Civil Rights Movement. *News Channel 3: WREG Online*. Retrieved from http://wreg.com/2012/05/17/some-black-pastors-in-memphis-oppose-president-obamas-position-on-same-sex-marriage/

Collins, P. H. (1990) *Black feminist thought: Knowledge, consciousness and politics of empowerment*. New York: Routledge.

Collins, P. H. (2001). "What's in a name? Womanism, Feminism and Beyond." *Black Scholar*, 26(1), 9–17.

Decter, M., Stanton Evans, M., Falwell, J., et al. Sex and God in American politics: A symposium. *Policy Review* (June 1984), 12–31.

Foucault, M. (1980). *The history of sexuality. Volume 1: An introduction*. (R. Hurley, trans.). New York: Vintage. (Original work published in 1976)

Garber, Eric. 1990. "A spectacle in color: The lesbian and gay subculture of jazz age Harlem." In M. Duberman, M. Vicinus, & G. Chauncey (Eds.), *Hidden from History: Reclaiming the Gay and Lesbian Past*, (pp. 318–331). New York: Penguin.

Halperin, D. M. (2003).The normalization of queer theory. *Journal of Homosexuality*, 45(2–4), 339–343.

Jagose, A. (1996) *Queer Theory*. Retrieved from http://www.australianhumanitiesreview.org/archive/Issue-Dec-1996/jagose.html

Johnson, E. P. (2005). "Quare" studies and (almost) everything I know about queer studies I learned from my grandmother. In E. P. Johnson & M. G. Henderson (Eds.), *Black queer studies: A queer anthology* (pp. 124–157). Durham, NC: Duke University Press.

Lee, W. (2003). Kuaering queer theory: My autocritography and a race-conscious, womanist, transnational turn. *Journal of Homosexuality*, 59(2–4), 147–170. Retrieved from http://uc.summon.serialssolutions.com/search?s.q=Lee%2C+Wenshu

Lorde, A. (1984). *Sister outsider*. New York: Crossing Press.

Morland, I. (2007). The limit of queer theory. *GLQ: A Journal of Lesbian and Gay Studies*, 13(4), 597–599.

Moore, M. R. (2006).Lipstick or Timberlands? Meanings of gender presentation in Black lesbian communities. *Signs*, 32(1), 113–139.

Murray, S. O. (1996) *American gay*. Chicago, IL: University of Chicago Press.

Namaste, K. (1994). The politics of inside/out: Queer theory, poststructuralism, and sociological approach to sexuality. *Sociological Theory*, 12(2), 220–231.

Phan, K. T. (2011, February 27). Christian Broadcasters Urged to Fight "Gay Is the New Black" Agenda. *Christian Post*. Retrieved from http://www. christianpost.com/news/ christian-broadcasters-urged-to-fight-gay-is-the-new-black-agenda-49196/

Richie, B., (1985). Battered Black women: A challenge for the Black community. *The Black Scholar*, XVI (2), 41-42.

Rofes, E. E. (1998). *Dry bones breathe: Gay men creating post-AIDS identities and cultures.* Binghamton, NY: Haworth Press.

Sapinoso, J. V. (2009). *From "quare" to "kweer": Towards a queer Asian American critique.* Retrieved from Proquest Digital Dissertations. (304920849).

Sedgwick, E. K. (1990). *The epistemology of the closet.* Berkeley: University of California Press.

Stone, A. L., & Ward, J. (2011). From 'Black people are not a homosexual act' to 'gay is the new Black': Mapping white uses of Blackness in modern gay rights campaigns in the United States. *Social Identities, 17*(5), 605-624.

Tally, J. (1986). Why "womanism"? The genesis of a new word and what it means. *Revista de Filología de la Universidad de La Laguna*, (5), 205-222.

Teunis, N. (2007). Sexual objectification and the construction of whiteness in the gay male community. *Culture, health & sexuality, 9*(3), 263-275.

Walker, A. (1983). *In search of our mothers' gardens: Womanist prose.* San Diego, CA: Harcourt Brace Jovanovich.

Warner, M. (Ed.). (1993). *Fear of a queer planet: Queer politics and social theory.* Minneapolis: University of Minnesota Press.

Whitlock, R. (2010). Getting queer: Teacher education, gender studies, and the cross-disciplinary quest for queer pedagogies. *Issues in Teacher Education, 19*(2), 81-104.

Womanism. (2005). In D. Dickson-Carr (Ed.). *Columbia Guide to contemporary African American Fiction.* New York: Columbia University Press, (pp. 230-232).

CHAPTER 3

The Emergence of the Black Queer Identity Matrix

In this chapter I analyze the multiple intersecting identities of the Black lesbian, female population through the use of photo feedback. Black lesbian females are minorities on three counts: race, gender, and sexual orientation; thus, there is limited research that focuses on the complexity of identity, identity dimensions, experiences, and perceptions of this population. This chapter serves as an exploratory research study in understanding what it means to be a Black lesbian, female in the United States through the theoretical framework of standpoint theory and intersectionality as well as the interpretive methodology of photo analysis (see Samuels, 2004), which I term "photo feedback analysis."

Standpoint theory asserts that everyday people possess knowledge different from that of those in power (West & Turner, 2010). Standpoints come from resisting those in power and refusing to accept the way society defines their group (West & Turner). Thus, this chapter provides a baseline of knowledge around what it means to be a Black lesbian, female in the United States; through the lens of the in-group. The complexity of these multiple intersecting identities will be expounded upon through photo feedback analysis, which is the use of a thematic analysis of photos taken by participants. Finally, this chapter concludes by moving toward an integrated theory of sexuality around Black queer identity, which is the title of this book: *Black Queer Identity Matrix*.

Overview

Black lesbians are relatively invisible in our society (see Howard & Lewis, 2011). Despite popular stereotypes, we know very little about their lives (Mays & Cochran, 1986). This pilot study seeks to serve as a catalyst to filling this void. Race relation's research, particularly with Black Americans, is abundant; however, social scientists have yet to explore the intersectionality of Black lesbian woman to any great extent. Black lesbian women embody social identities that pose a variety of challenges for researchers (Bowleg, 2008). Specifically, social identities and inequality are interdependent for groups such as Black lesbians, not mutually exclusive (see Bowleg, 2008). In short, researchers must be careful not to minimize the multiple intersecting identities of Black lesbians by treating their identities as additive (Black + lesbian + woman) versus intersectional (Black lesbian woman) (Bowleg). This study approaches intersectionality research from the perspective that ordinary people who live at the crux of structural inequality based on intersections of race, gender, and sexual orientation hold significant promise in helping to create a body of knowledge around the complexities of being a Black lesbian female—a minority on three counts.

Many of the approaches to the study of Black lesbian women can be found in the field of psychology (Bowleg, 2008; Cochran & Mays, 1994). Much of the empirical literature on this community focuses on three primary areas: intimate relationships, coping mechanisms, and mental health (Cochran & Mays; Hall & Greene, 2002; Bowleg, 2008). This study seeks to further develop the literature by gaining insight into the triple identity experiences of this group by utilizing an intersectional approach in which participants are able to describe their multiple intersecting identities without being forced to disaggregate identities. Thus, participants in this study will be able to share their identities in the way it best resonates with them.

Due to the exploratory nature of this study it is projected that valuable insights will be discovered along the lines of social inequalities and social identities of this group, thus enabling practitioners, policymakers, and researchers to begin to assess and understand the characteristics, desires, expectations, needs, and demands of the Black lesbian female community. Specifically, this study seeks to answer the following research questions:

1. What do the images submitted by the participants ask the audience to believe, understand, feel, and/or think?
2. How do Black lesbian, women resist power structures?
3. How have social systems shaped Black lesbian, female identity?
4. What fundamental social, economic, political, and/or cultural interests do these images reflect?

The Value of Images

We use images to "understand, describe, and define the world as we see it" (Sturken & Cartwright, 2009, p. 12). Thus, images are vital in constructing meaning about the world around us, which is the impetus of this study. More specifically, the camera records the décor of everyday life; the photographic image is capable of directing attention across a field of gestures, interaction rituals, social types, political styles, artistic motifs, cultural norms, and other signs as they intersect in any event (Hariman & Lucaites, 2003). Photography has been regarded as a more objective practice than, say, painting or drawing (Sturken & Cartwright) due to its more positivist nature.

Positivism, a philosophy that emerged in the mid-nineteenth century, holds that scientific knowledge is the only authentic knowledge and concerns itself with truths about the world (Sturken & Cartwright, 2009). Hence, in positivism, machines (i.e., cameras) were regarded as more reliable than unaided human sensory perception of the hand of the artist (i.e., drawing) (Sturken & Cartwright).

Photography seemed to suit the positivist way of thinking because it is a method of producing representations through a mechanical recording device (the camera) rather than the scientist's subjective eye and hand (Sturken & Cartwright, 2009). In the context of positivism, the photographic camera can be understood as a scientific tool for registering reality more accurately (Sturken & Cartwright). Thus, images can provide powerful and objective insights into the complexities of one's life.

The power of the image derives not only from its status as photographic evidence of [an] exact moment in time but also from its powerful evocation of the personal and political struggles of [an] era (Sturken & Cartwright, 2009). In short, the photograph has the capacity both to present evidence and to evoke a magical or mythical quality that moves us beyond specific empirical truths (Sturken & Cartwright), which provides the basis of my approach in this study.

Ronald Barthes uses the terms "denotative" and "connotative" to describe different kinds and levels of meaning produced at the same time and for the same viewers in the same photograph. An image can denote certain apparent truths, providing documentary evidence of objective circumstances. The denotative meaning of the image refers to its literal, explicit meaning. The same photograph may connote less explicit, more culturally specific associations and meanings, which is germane to this study. "Connotative meanings are informed by cultural and historical contexts of the image" and the "lived, felt knowledge of those circumstances—all that the image means to a person personally and socially" (Sturken & Cartwright, 2009. p. 20). Consequently, I expect to gain valuable cultural and social knowledge of this population as well as provide the public with a baseline of knowledge around its needs, values, and motifs; thus, this study significantly contributes to the Black lesbian community as well as provides a broadening of knowledge for the public at large. This is important due to the lack of Black lesbian visibility within mainstream media, literature, and politics today.

Black Female Representation

"Representation" refers to the use of language and images to create meaning about the world around us (Sturken & Cartwright, 2009). Hence, the increased visibility of the gay and lesbian community in the twenty-first-century mainstream media is significant in influencing public interest and understanding of the gay and lesbian community, as well as the economic, political, and cultural interests of the gay and lesbian community.

There is an obvious underrepresentation of Black lesbian females in mainstream media; thus, we know very little about Black lesbians. The Showtime series *The L Word*, which aired between 2004 and 2009, was a fairly popular show that focused on the lesbian experience. However, the program's cast was predominately White, with one African American character (Tasha) appearing in the program (Howard & Lewis, 2011). Tasha's appearance on the show was problematic because she was a Black female minor character within a predominately White cast; consequently Tasha acted White, had a White significant other, and had no Black friends. Thus, experiences relevant or specific to the Black lesbian community as well as Black lesbian identity were incessantly invalidated or rendered nonexistent within this popular medium. According to Shockley (1983), "No efforts [have been] made by knowledgeable individuals who could . . . document truth over myths to help others recognize the Black lesbian as a person, not a thing" (p. 85). This study seeks to offer valuable insights into the identity dimensions of the Black lesbian community as well as provide visibility.

Representations of Black women in mainstream media constitute a tradition of distorted and limited imagery (Bobo, 1995). Bobo states that dating back to the earliest years of media, "Black women have been presented as sexually deviant; as the dominating matriarchal figure; as strident, eternally ill-tempered wenches; and as wretched victims" (p. 33). More recently, Stephens and Phillips (2003) identified these images as Jezebel, Mammy, Matriarch, and Welfare Mother. These images provide the public with a distorted and problematic view of Black female identity. In their work Stephens and Phillips present these four images as the foundation for contemporary African American female sexual scripts that are often reflected in hip-hop media as Freak, Golddigger, Diva, Dyke, Gangster Bitch, Sister Savior, Earth Mother, and Baby Mama. Such depictions of Black women are not above suspicion. These images represent Black women as less than human and "useful commodities in a very serious power struggle" (Bobo, p. 36). These images are destructive and do not present an identity that is reflective of the Black female community.

Researchers should participate in a social activism that aids in positively affecting the lives of Black women (Howard & Lewis, 2011). Bobo (1995) asserts that "the task of the critic within the interpretive community is to give voice to those who are usually never considered in any analysis of cultural works" (p. 51). The goal of the researcher is to develop "strategic interpretations" of audience activity, for, according to Ang (1989), "what is at stake is a politics of interpretation" (p. 105). This study offers participants—Black lesbian women—an opportunity to speak back to these representations (or lack thereof) by offering the reader a more authentic representation of the Black female community, which Bobo (1995) implores.

Standpoint Theory and Intersectionality

Ultimately, this research is guided by two theoretical frameworks, which are *standpoint theory* and *intersectionality*. These theoretical frameworks allow for a more critical analysis of the complexity of triple jeopardy minorities as it relates to social systems and identity, which are fitting for this study. They will be discussed in turn.

Standpoint Theory

Based on the research of Nancy C. M. Hartsock, this study employs Standpoint Theory (ST). Standpoint Theory gives authority to people's own voices (West & Turner, 2010). This theoretical perspective is particularly suited for this study because it operates from the assumption that everyday people harbor vital knowledge as it relates to social systems, oppression, and power. Thus, due to the multiple oppressed identities of the Black lesbian community, I found this framework relevant in identifying valuable information around "resisting those in power and refusing to accept the way society defines their group" (Wood, 1994, p. 502). According to West and Turner:

> Standpoint Theory is built on knowledge generated from everyday lives of people—acknowledging that individuals' own perspectives are the most important sources of information about their experiences. (p. 502)

Germane to this study is the assumption of Standpoint Theory that "the potential understanding of the oppressed (the standpoint) makes visible the inhumanity of the existing relations among groups and moves us toward a better and more just world" (West & Turner, 2010, p. 506). This renders standpoint theory relevant for investigating the ways in which social systems shape their identities. In addition, this framework allowed me to investigate the messages that shape the participants standpoints or "the location shared by a group experiencing outsider status, within a social structure, that lends a particular kind of sense making to a persons lived experiences" (West & Turner, 2010, p. 508).

Most critiques around Standpoint Theory revolve around essentialism. Essentialism obscures the diversity that exists among women (West & Turner, 2010). This study focuses on the commonality of multiple oppressed identities (race, gender, and sexual orientation) while acknowledging various expressions of their common experience. There is no one fixed Black lesbian identity.

Collins (1990) asserts that varied expressions derive from the diversity of class, region, age, and sexual orientation, which shape individual Black women's lives. Research, then, on Black women's lives, reactions to, and interpretations of [their lived experiences] will help to identify any themes related to Black women's collective perspectives, as well as their individual perspectives (Bobo, 1995). In short, I hypothesize that standpoint theory is valuable in examining the multiple oppressed identities of Black lesbians in the United States by aiding in a critical examination of dominance and power within the social hierarchy.

Intersectionality

As discussed in chapter 1, intersectionality research focuses on the integrated multiple oppressed identities typically relevant to marginalized groups of research participants who have been historically silenced or invisible (Warner, 2008). Each of the numerous identities that comprise the person will uniquely contribute to the holistic lived experience of the individual in ways that cannot be completely or accurately captured by examining any one of the identities in isolation (Bowleg, 2008; Brah & Phoenix, 2004). Thus, this study does not treat the Black lesbian identity as additive but rather a complex identity that is interrelated.

Intersectionality research is inherently complex and methodologically varied, the scope of which is beyond the objectives of the current chapter; however, such research has been discussed extensively by feminist scholars in the field of women's studies (McCall, 2005). Much intersectionality research has focused on uncovering connections among systems of oppression. The paradigm of intersectionality addresses any specific social location where these identities meet or intersect to produce a distinctive or unique group history or experience (Howard & Lewis, 2011). From the premise of intersectionality research, Black lesbians can be expected to perceive their identities along the lines of social, political, and perhaps economic inequalities. Thus, research on the intersecting multiple oppressed identities of Black lesbians residing in the United States is valuable in that the Black female lesbian identity remains fairly invisible in various facets of society, including but not limited to politics and popular culture. This study seeks to create a baseline of knowledge around this identity.

Purpose

The current research is designed to explore the social identities within and across the Black lesbian female community through the use of reflexive photography. Specifically, this study's objectives are to answer the following research questions:

1. What do the images submitted by participants ask the audience to believe, understand, feel, and/or think?
2. How do Black lesbian women resist power structures?
3. How have social systems shaped Black lesbian female identity?
4. What fundamental social, economic, political, and/or cultural interests do these images reflect?

Method

The method used in this study is termed "photo feedback analysis." Methods similar to this have not been consistently used in the communication field; however, it has been used in various academic disciplines. In current literature, "photovoice" is the name of the method employed by researchers who use photos and feedback to gather information on communities. The term "photovoice" was originally proposed by Wang and Burris in the early 1990s to describe the approach of blending narrative with photography to explore community issues; however, this methodology builds on a deep historical foundation of individuals and communities blending images and words to express needs, history, culture, problems, and desires (Collier & Collier, 1986; Pink, 2001). Photovoice involves participants sharing photographs in a group setting guided by a session moderator who facilitates group discussion around key photographs. This information has traditionally been used to share information with policymakers (see Wang, 1999). In recent years, photovoice has gained popularity as a qualitative research method that permits researchers from various disciplines to visualize individuals' perceptions about their everyday realities (Close, 2007). Photovoice has been used to study a variety of communities, cultures, and ethnicities and to explore a range of factors relating to health and social inquiry (Wang & Pies, 2004). Photovoice is particularly useful for participants as it provides an opportunity to visually portray experiences and share personal knowledge about particular issues that may be difficult to express with words alone (Wang & Burris, 1997). The current study employs photo feedback analysis, which is a culmination of photovoice and thematic analysis. Thematic analysis will be expanded upon in the qualitative inquiry section.

This small-scale exploratory study utilized 25 images accompanied by one to two paragraph typed descriptions submitted by 5 human subjects between the ages of 24 and 50, who self-identified as Black lesbian women. The photo feedback analysis method was used in order to understand the perceptions of the Black lesbian population as it relates to their complex identity. Photo feedback is a form of photo elicitations where written feedback is given based upon the viewing of a particular photograph (Sampson-Cordle, 2001). Although photo research methods have been around since the early twentieth century, the methodology is only now slowly gaining interest for use in research studies (Sampson-Cordle). In this study, the participants took photographs and provided typed descriptions of each photo, which I then analyzed using thematic analysis. This approach allowed the participants to take photographs on their own time and free from researcher influence.

After gaining Institutional Review Board (IRB) approval, participants were recruited during the spring of 2011 using lesbian-oriented networking websites, lesbian-oriented social events, and word of mouth. Prescreening was completed via the phone and in person in order to ensure that the participants were self-described Black lesbian women over the age of 18.

The selected participants were given an introductory letter that provided important details of the study. In this letter respondents were informed of the study's purpose and importance. Each participant was asked to take digital photographs of 5 unique ideas that symbolize "what it means to be a Black lesbian female in America." Participants were informed that photographs could include but were not limited to any item, place, or physical characteristic. Participants were also informed that people could be included in the photographs; however, it was asked that they only be used as part of a larger concept and that the people in the photographs should not be recognizable. In other words, photos of people should focus on activities or events they are participating in rather than just a person, and people in the images should not be able to be identified.

Participants were then informed that once the photos were taken, they were required to write a one or two paragraph comment on all photos to explain what each photo meant to them in terms of being a Black lesbian woman in America. This provided a better idea of why they found it relevant for the study. Once completed, participants were instructed to upload and email photographs to me.

In order to adhere to the ethical requirements for social scientific inquiry using human participants, I used consent forms that allowed participants full permission to withdraw from the study at any point. In addition, the participants were granted full anonymity in all published reports. The names in this study are all pseudonyms.

Participants also signed the form for researcher permission to use their submitted photos in anyway deemed necessary as it relates to the completion and publishing of this study.

Photo feedback analysis, described here, has not been used in communication research, and any methodological inquiry similar has not been termed photo feedback analysis. In conducting this study, it became evident to me that this type of methodological inquiry revealed a sort of "meta" experience for my participants, meaning the method elicited how the participants felt upon reflection of their experiences and identity. This method naturally involves a heightened degree of self-awareness and reflection, which is evident as you continue to read the following sections.

Data Collection

Photos and drawings have always played an important role in teaching and learning (Strickland, Keats, & Marinak, 2010). More specifically, photo elicitation methods are a growing means of data collection that provide more depth and meaning to participant responses (Samuels, 2004). Additionally, using photographs as a research tool has recently began to gain attention in scholarship and has proven valuable (see Strickland, Keats, & Marinak;

Samuels). There is a wide range of methodological approaches in regards to utilizing photography as a means of data collection; accordingly studies that utilize the photo feedback approach harbor the common theme of allowing participants to share their present thoughts and appeal to their own backgrounds and previous experiences by visually reflecting their culture and social class. Harper (1988) states, "In the reflexive photographic method the subject shares in the definition of meaning; thus the definitions are said to 'reflect back' from the subject" (pp. 64–65). Hence, this approach is fitting to discovering identity dimensions and authentic experiences and reflections within the Black lesbian community.

In this study, data collection consisted of participants taking digital photographs with their own cameras as part of the inquiry process and accompanying each photo with a one or two paragraph write-up of what the photo meant to them in terms of being a Black lesbian woman in America. Participants were given one month to take photos and submit them to the researcher via email. Thematic analysis was used to code and analyze the data.

Qualitative Analysis

Utilizing thematic analysis is a five-step process. First, the researcher needs to familiarize him- or herself with the data by transcribing, reading, and rereading the data while simultaneously noting initial ideas (Howard & Lewis, 2011). Second, the researcher needs to generate initial codes by noting interesting features of the data in a systematic fashion across the entire dataset and then by collating data relevant to each code. Third, the researcher needs to search for themes by collating codes into potential themes and gathering all data relevant to each potential theme (Braun & Clarke, 2006). Fourth, the researcher needs to check if the themes relate to the project's research question(s). Fifth, the researcher defines and names the themes. Clear and definitive themes need to be generated, as this serves to outline the overall story discovered by the analysis.

The photos and feedback submitted by participants were coded using the aforementioned method—thematic analysis. Thematic analysis does not just describe data; it provides a more comprehensive and nuanced account of themes, or a group of themes, within the data.

Results

The findings of this study provide insight into Black lesbian identity, ideological considerations and implications of this understudied group, as well as the social, cultural, and historical meaning of symbols within the Black lesbian community. Several themes emerged in the analysis of participant responses. In this investigation the responses represent diversity across and within the African American lesbian participants within the study, yet common threads were present. This section expounds upon those common threads.

Themes were extracted by coding and collating initial codes examined through photos taken by participants and the transcription of text data provided by participants. Using thematic analysis of the photos and feedback, the following themes emerged from participant responses: (1) Representation, (2) Black Queer Identity Matrix, (3) Empowerment, and (4) Coexistence. It is noteworthy to mention that not all photos submitted by participants are included in this chapter. Some photos did not fit the aforementioned themes and therefore are not included.

Standpoint theory allows scholars to operate from the assumption that everyday people harbor vital knowledge as it relates to social systems, oppression, and power. This framework also allows for the identification of valuable information around "resisting those in power and refusing to accept the way society defines their group" (Wood, 1994, p. 502). Thus, responses and photos from participants allow for the examination and analysis of cultural, economic, and political messages that may be in opposition of the larger dominate society.

Theme 1: Representation

Responses across the data set reflect an interest in the Black lesbian community making the public aware of the varied gender expressions within the community. Thus, this theme encompasses the spectrum of lesbian identity as it relates to gender expression as opposed to the stereotypical representations so often portrayed in the media. Responses reflect a sophisticated awareness of, and concern for, how media products—and public perception—are often constructed as limited images of this marginalized group. This exhibits the ways in which social systems, such as the media and public opinion, attempt to shape Black lesbian female identity; however, this research has found that Black lesbian females are varied and diverse in their gender expression, which addresses research question 3 (RQ3) (How have social systems shaped Black lesbian female identity?). This theme also addresses RQ1 (What do the images submitted by participants ask the audience to believe, understand, feel, and/or think?).

Kelly states, "Lesbianism is often viewed as a fad or something that some hope will go away . . . [thus] sometimes relationships are portrayed in the media as fleeting and emphasis [is placed on] promiscuity." This sentiment is represented by figure 3.1, a vivid image of aged hands overlapping one another accompanied by matching wedding bands.

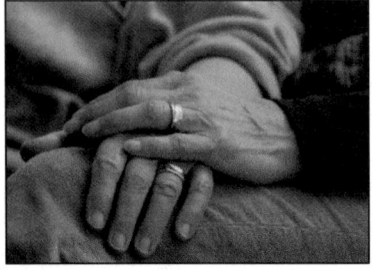

Figure 3.1

Thus, of importance to Black lesbian women within this data set is the notion that lesbian love and identity are stable—not fleeting or contemplative. Hence, as it relates to RQ1 (What do the images submitted by participants ask the audience to believe, understand, feel, and/or think?), participants ask the audience to consider social systems, such as media outlets, that do not provide images or archetypes depicting stable Black lesbian relationships, which have the power to influence Black lesbian females' sense of self. For example, one participant, Kelly, goes on to say, "[In this photo] I wanted to represent younger people who are in love and are comfortable demonstrating their love for each other."

Even as more media programming incorporates gay and lesbian characters, relationships, and storylines of healthy Black lesbians, love is rendered absent, symbolically sending a message that it does not exist or that it is invalid.

An interesting attribute depicted in figure 3.2 is the young lesbians portrayed in the image represent the butch-femme dichotomy that is often found in the Black lesbian community (see Moore, 2006). One female is more masculine, evidenced by her loose fitting clothing and braided hair; her lover projects a more traditional feminine appearance. This butch-femme dichotomy is pervasive within the Black lesbian community and reflects the heteronormative presentation of male to female relationships or masculine to feminine. This butch-femme dichotomy is elaborated on in chapter 4 of this volume.

Figure 3.2

Black women take very careful pains to consistently present the same type of gender display because they are looking to create a particular aesthetic self and because the norms of the community require a consistency in their gender presentation (Moore, 2006). Thus, social systems have shaped Black lesbian relationships. The structure imposed by community social norms becomes problematic when it impedes a person's freedom to partner with someone who has the *wrong* gender display (Moore).

The butch-femme dichotomy, as well as the spectrum of Black female expression, is reinforced by another participant. Veronica states, "I have moved along the spectrum from being more butch to more femme." Kelly reiterates this notion of varied gender expressions within the lesbian community:

> Lesbians come in all stripes. Overwhelmingly, the image of lesbian is that butch or dominant masculine gender woman. I wanted to demonstrate (in figure 3.3) that lesbian women cover the spectrum represented here by their shoe selections.

Figure 3.3

This theme, based on participant responses, speaks back to the representations of lesbians found in various media outlets and provides vital information from everyday people about their lived experiences, which standpoint theory seeks to accomplish. Thus, we are able to realize "the location shared by a group (Black lesbian females) experiencing outsider status, within a social structure, that lends a particular kind of sense making to one's lived experiences" (West & Turner, 2010, p. 508). Consequently, this theme teaches us that Black lesbians long to see more varied gender representations or more authentic images of Black lesbian women in the media that represent the complexity of gender expression and fluidity of the community. In addition, we see that Black lesbian relationships are constrained by the performance of gender roles in which there is a masculine-feminine dichotomy that is largely adhered to in the Black lesbian community.

Theme 2: Black Queer Identity Matrix

The data revealed various subtleties of homophobia, sexism, racism, oppression, and disconfirmation in which the Black lesbian female has become accustomed to coping. as well as creating coping mechanisms to speak back to society's cultural norms of oppression, which I term "Black Queer Identity Matrix" due to the various forms of discrimination weighted on the triple minority identity of the Black lesbian female. The amalgamation of intersectionality impregnated by the Black lesbian female identity is the core of the Black Queer Identity Matrix. The culmination of data revealed various coping mechanisms enacted by the participants as well as communicative dynamics that serve as viable functions in speaking back to ideological hegemony within a society that pushes triple jeopardy individuals to the margins. Consequently, this theme addresses RQ2 (How do Black lesbian women resist power structures?), RQ3 (How have social systems shaped Black lesbian female identity?), and RQ4 (What fundamental social, economic, political and/or cultural interests do these images reflect?).

Amber depicts the complexity of being a minority on three counts by providing a picture of a Black teddy bear being a minority, surrounded by rolls of toilet paper, which represent the majority.

Figure 3.4

As it relates to this image, Amber states:

> To be a Black lesbian female in America means you are three times the minority. Born a woman in America makes you a minority, born black in America makes you a minority, and being a lesbian in American makes you a minority. To be all three simply magnifies this identity. If anyone paints a picture of America, a Black lesbian female does not "fit the script." It doesn't matter how nice or intelligent you are, how many degrees or accolades you have, bottom line is, we are the poster children of what it is to be a minority in America.

Figure 3.4 is also a powerful depiction of how the Black lesbian female does not fit into the fabric of American society due to her triple jeopardy identities. Amber's reflections illuminate the distinction that emerges at the intersection where sexual orientation meets cultural, ethnic, and racial variables. This sentiment also reveals that multiple oppressed identities should not be desegregated but work together as a matrix of oppression—a Black Queer Identity Matrix.

There are social and political constructs in which identity produces power in America. For example, Amber states, "To be a Black lesbian female in America means life will not be easy. . . . In America, it is hard to be just Black, just female, or just a lesbian; to be all three is overwhelming." Amber continues, "Every day you wake up, you have three strikes against you"; revealing the struggle inherent within this identity as well as revealing the psychological toll one's identity can have on mental health.

Consequently, health disparities within the Black lesbian community also emerged within the data. Health disparities are tied intimately into economic power in which Black lesbian women as a group do not possess. Kelly perceives that there are health disparities that affect the Black lesbian community. Kelly asserts, "Lesbians disproportionately have poorer health care." She accompanies this assertion with a photo of the AIDS button.

Figure 3.5

As more thoroughly discussed in chapter 1, historically, health data collection efforts have not specifically included the Black lesbian population; as a result it can be difficult to gather information regarding the specific health needs of the Black lesbian community. Some data specifically relevant to the Black lesbian community is available in the *American Journal of Public Health* and other health-related journals. However, a review of 3.8 million citations of articles in the National Library of Medicine published between 1980 and 1999 found that just 3,800 (0.1%) related to LGBTQ issues. Of these articles, 2,300 (61%) were disease specific, with a focus on sexually transmitted diseases, mostly HIV/AIDS. Moreover, 85% of the articles failed to include any mention of the racial or ethnic background of the individuals studied. However, with the advent of recent research, there are huge health disparities within the LGBTQ community and consequently within the LGBTQ of color community that need to be addressed. In addition to health inequalities discussed by the participants, religion also emerged as a factor within the Black Queer Identity Matrix, which adds a layer of homophobia for some Black lesbians.

As found in previous studies, including the current one, religion is an important factor within the Black community in which homophobia is often fueled by the Black church. Within many Black communities the church plays a significant role in the production of homophobia, although it is important to recognize that Black churches are not the only source of homophobia in Black communities (Ward, 2005). Homophobia exists in many cultures and subcultures around the globe; however, the Black church in the United States is widely recognized as the central, oldest, and most influential institution in the Black community (Lincoln & Mamiya, 1990). This is detrimental and poses a threat to the psychological, mental, and intellectual liberation and health of the Black community as it relates to unity. For example, Kelly states,

> This photo [figure 3.6] represents my own struggle with religion and lesbian identity. This particular church is affirming, but most churches, especially African American churches, are not tolerant. There is a struggle between faith and sexual orientation. However, many Blacks grow up in the church and view it as a key part of who they are despite their sexual orientation.

Thus, religion often adds a layer of struggle for some Black lesbian women as the church is an integral part of the Black community. The role of the church within African American history is unique in that the civil rights movement of the 1950s started in the Black church. The leadership role of Black churches in the civil rights movement was a natural extension of the community and served as a center for political activism, community, as well as support. Thus, the Black church is integral within Black cultural memory.

THE EMERGENCE OF THE BLACK QUEER IDENTITY MATRIX

Figure 3.6

In short, race, gender, and sexual orientation intersect in the lives of Black lesbian women, creating distinct complexities (or a matrix), such as religion and health disparities, in which one is forced to struggle with in America.

In accordance with the intersectionality literature, women's identities of race, gender, and sexuality are not likely to be compartmentalized (Bowleg, 2008; McCall, 2005), but they work together as interdependent identities. These distinct complexities bring rise to the need for the Black lesbian female to encompass strength, resiliency, and pride. This concept will be further explicated in the following theme.

Theme 3: Empowerment

This theme encompasses the characteristics of pride, strength, and power. This theme is defined as the ability, as well as struggle, to exist and overcome internal and external fears through acceptance of self, solidarity, and affirmation. Several participants discussed the necessity of loving oneself and empowering oneself through the use of visual rhetoric or mental empowerment in order to cope with the power structures within the American fabric. Pride is a source of resisting power structures. This theme speaks to RQ2 (How do Black lesbian women resist power structures?).

Amber states, "To be a Black lesbian female in America means you must be strong, one cannot be a Black lesbian female and be weak. Being a Black woman in America is hard enough, but to also be a lesbian you must have strength." Figure 3.7 reflects the idea of being mentally strong as opposed to physically strong. Mentally strong, for the participants, means to be proud of what one represents—proud of who you are. Amber states, "Pride is necessary to survive" as a Black lesbian woman.

Figure 3.7

The importance of pride is demonstrated in the following narrative. Victoria recounts a story in which she and her girlfriend got kicked out of a diner for kissing. Victoria later organized a protest with the Lesbian Avengers and the Anti-Violence Project in front of the diner. She states:

Within hours (a day or two) we had a picket line going, had organized a "kiss in" action at the diner, where women stood up and kissed after singing "You must remember this, a kiss is just a kiss." And giving out Hershey kisses and literature about the incident to by passers on the street.

This theme shows that solidarity brings a sense of empowerment to the Black lesbian community. This sense of solidarity and acceptance enables Black lesbian women to overcome internal and external fears within an oppressive society. Victoria continues, "It felt wildly powerful to be connected to so many lesbians and to effect change. The owners apologized on camera."

Thus, significant to Black lesbian women is a sense of empowerment, experienced through solidarity, mental strength, and symbolic power. For example, Taylor provides a picture of a wife beater undershirt. She states, "The wife beater picture relates to me because to me it's a symbol of strength and power." Taylor goes on to associate power with masculinity:

Because your muscles are out and having muscles and a certain physical stature gives you a sense of power and a dominating confidence. I will say wife beaters are masculine as well and as you know in this world to many people, being masculine automatically gives you power, strength, prestige, and a sense of dominance. So if you rock a wife beater you may feel more powerful that day.

This further demonstrates the societal structures inherent within the female psyche—the unequal power structures embedded in one's consciousness; structures that identify masculinity with power and femininity with weakness. Standpoint Theory seeks to understand the influence that a particular location exerts on people's views of the world and on their communication (West & Turner, 2010). In this theme, the Black lesbian shares that she feels masculinity is empowering, and the visual persuasion Taylor enacts in exerting power is the wearing of a wife beater.

Theme 4: Coexistence

One subtle yet significant theme across the data set was the notion of *coexistence*. This theme is defined as learning to live together, accept difference, and make the world a safe place for difference. The importance of "others" and the acknowledgment that others exist was an overwhelming characteristic across the data set and addresses RQ3 (How have social systems shaped Black lesbian female identity?) and RQ4 (What fundamental social, economic, political, and/or cultural interests do these images reflect?).

Isabella states:

Out of all my tattoos, I must say that this is one is my favorite tattoo. The definition of Coexist is to live in peace with one another or others despite differences, especially as a matter of policy. The Coexist symbol stands for coexistence among people who practice different religions and people who have different points of view. (See figure 3.9.)

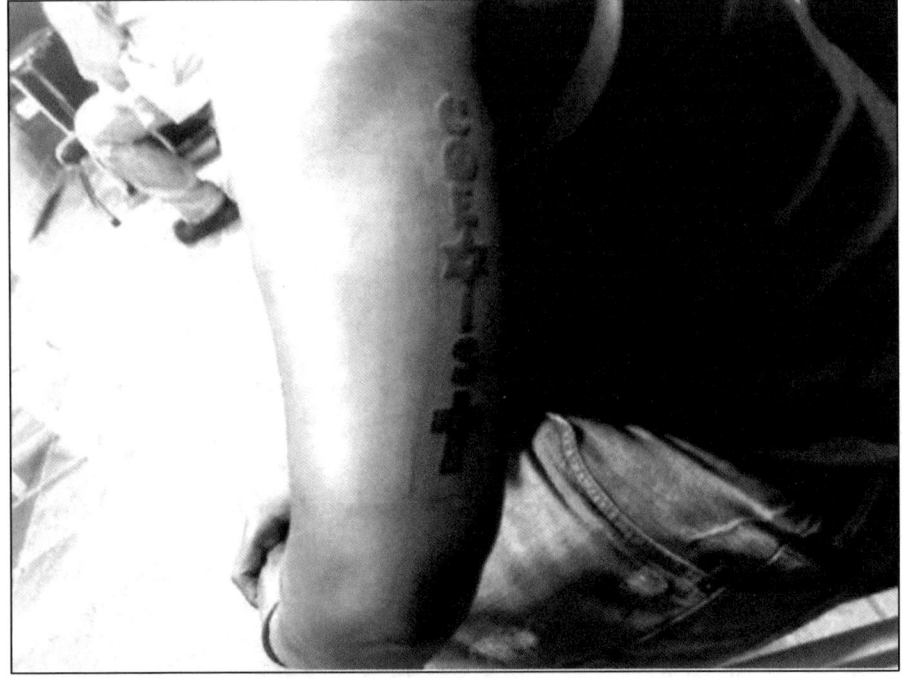

Figure 3.9

One concern for the LGBTQ (lesbian, gay, bisexual, transgender, questioning) community is the possibility of discrimination or ostracism due to one's sexual orientation and "coming out" as a lesbian. Unfortunately, this theme shows that social systems have rendered Black lesbian women as outcasts. Isabella asserts:

> Being a homosexual, I know how it feels to be an outcast and how people will kick me out of their life, just because of my lifestyle. One day I wish that people will be able to live together without anger and conflict despite anyone or anything being different.

This theory of difference discussed by participants is well documented by Black lesbian poet and scholar Audre Lorde. Lorde suggests it is not our differences that divide us. It is our inability to recognize, accept, and celebrate those differences (Lorde, 1984). Differences in race, sexuality, religion, and so on should be celebrated and a reason for growth as opposed to destruction.

This growth can only come when we are able to coexist within a culture composed of multiple layers and complexities.

The Black lesbian female is rendered to outside status in a society that privileges White male heterosexuality. This theme illuminates the standpoint of the Black lesbian female by acknowledging her struggle with difference within American culture. The central concept of the standpoint theory is a location, shared by a group experiencing outsider status, within the social structure that lends a particular kind of sense making to a person's lived experience (West & Turner, 2010).

Conclusion

As demonstrated throughout this chapter, African American lesbian responses are diverse, yet they share common threads. The various responses across the dataset reflect the notion that it is vital to generate knowledge from the everyday lives of people in order to understand systems of power and how those systems shape communication. Consequently, standpoint theory provides a theoretical framework in which researchers begin with the marginalized, focusing on their stories and interpretations (West & Turner, 2010), which this study seeks to do. The concepts of voice, speaking out, and speaking for others are important to standpoint theory and standpoint epistemology, and they are all concepts rooted in communication (West & Turner). This study makes readers aware of the ways in which the Black lesbian community resists those in power by encompassing the characteristics of pride, strength, and power through organizing protests, wearing clothes that are deemed empowering, and staying mentally strong. Additionally, this study illuminates the ways in which the structures of power serve to dominate and oppress individuals who are not in positions of power. For example, participants reflected on the complexity of being a minority on three counts and having an identity that does not "fit the script." Thus, this study provides us with a glimpse of social life around these individuals who are members of the Black lesbian community. Standpoint theory suggests that there can be no single view of social life, as it is influenced by the position one occupies. This study provides a baseline of knowledge around how discussants in this study view their social life. It is clear that the multiple intersecting identities of discussants in this study largely influence their social life.

Intersectionality provides a theoretical framework in which researchers are able to examine the interdependency of multiple identities. Each of the numerous identities that comprise the person will uniquely contribute to the holistic lived experience of the individual in ways that cannot be completely or accurately captured by examining any one of the identities in isolation (Bowleg, 2008; Brah & Phoenix, 2004). Thus, this study has illuminated that discussants find themselves in a Black Queer Identity Matrix in which these individuals seek to coexist and be accepted as members within a society that has in many ways marginalized them. For example, one participant reflected on her tattoo, which reads *coexist*. In America, tattoos are thought of by many as a cultural statement which, for most people, has significant personal meaning. American culture is said to be a melting pot of various identities, identities that also include members of the LGBTQ community, thus tolerance and acceptance is critical to the cultural interests of Americans.

Implications

In this study, intersectionality and standpoint theory combine to examine Black lesbian identity and what it means to be a Black lesbian female in America. Representation, Black Queer Identity Matrix, Empowerment, and Coexistence each emerged as themes across the data set.

The research found that Black lesbian women share in varied expressions of gender and live on a gender expression continuum. For example, stereotypical representations of lesbians in mass media do not account for the varied physical presentations in the actual Black lesbian community—the continuum represents very feminine expressions to very masculine expressions. This is important as we move toward an increase in gay-lesbian representations in the media.

This study also reiterated, as previous scholars have noted, the butch-femme dichotomy prevalent across Black female relationships in which there is a more feminine partner and more masculine partner in romantic relationships. This is symptomatic of the ways in which the social system of heteronormativity (re-creating male–female presentation in romantic relationships) have shaped Black lesbian identity (see Moore, 2006).

One significant finding demonstrates the Black lesbian female's experience with multiple forms of oppression all logged onto one cultural body. The implications here are that as a minority on three counts the Black lesbian female finds herself in a Black Queer Identity Matrix in which race, gender, and sexual orientation are interlocking systems of oppression. Thus, it becomes important for the Black lesbian female to implement oral, mental, and visual communication strategies as coping and resistance mechanisms such as visual forms of empowerment through the act of wearing a wife beater, organizing a protest against organizational heterosexism, or more mental coping mechanisms of gaining a sense of pride, which all emerged in this pilot study. These communication strategies as coping mechanisms should be further explored in future research as we examine the multiple intersecting identities of the Black queer community as well as the LGBTQ of color community. This will move us toward a more integrated theory of sexuality within queer research and theoretical frameworks that incorporate the variables of race, ethnicity, and culture that is lacking in the current state of scholarship around sexual orientation.

The ideas expressed by the population studied here are unique in that a baseline of knowledge is created around a population that is often understudied and left unrecognized in scholarship. People are situated in specific social locations; they occupy different places in the social hierarchy based on their membership in social groups (poor, wealthy, men, women, European American, African American, Latino, uneducated, well educated, and so forth). Because of these social locations, individuals view the social situation from particular vantage points. Those vantage points formed in opposition to those in power, resisting the social affiliation given to them by those in power, become standpoints. No standpoint allows a person to view the entire social situation completely—all standpoints are partial—but people on the lower rungs of the social hierarchy do see more than their own position (West & Turner, 2010, p. 504). Thus, the Black lesbian female as a minority on three counts is able to provide vital information around life from a particular social location, information in which politicians, researchers, writers, producers, and those with limited exposure to this population can learn from.

Limitation of Study

Though this study creates a baseline of valuable knowledge around the Black lesbian community, there are some limitations that should be discussed in order to encourage more research around Black lesbian identity and particularly to encourage more research utilizing photo feedback analysis. Ideally, the identification of these limitations will lead to subsequent attention and ultimately improved effectiveness.

There is no notable research that uses the photo feedback method as employed here. Though the method provides a meta-analysis in which photos provide connotative and denotative texture to findings and analysis as well as symbolic meanings revealed through images, this method has not been utilized and adequately developed within the field of communication studies. This method produced a total of 25 images submitted by 5 participants, producing a larger amount of photos or data within the data set than the number participants. Thus, this study cannot be generalized beyond what has been found around the individuals who participated in this study. Thus, more research should be conducted in order to address other segments of the Black lesbian community so that more in-depth data can be discovered around the social identities of Black lesbian women. Finally, this study did not take into consideration other identities that may influence the meaning of being a Black lesbian woman in America. For example, there was no distinction in the study between who was out or in the closet as a lesbian. This is potentially a vital variable that could influence aspects such as, but not limited to, empowerment and representation. In addition, other intersecting identities were not teased out, such as religion, age, and social class, among others that may be valuable in understanding various segments of the Black lesbian community. It is my hope that these limitations can be addressed in subsequent studies that focus on the LGBTQ community of color.

Bibliography

Ang, I. (1989). Wanted audiences: On the politics of empirical audience studies. In E. Seiter (Ed.), *Remote control: Television, audiences, and cultural power* (pp. 96-115). London: Routledge.

Bobo, J. (1995). *Black women as cultural readers*. New York: Columbia University Press.

Bowleg, L. (2008). When Black + lesbian + woman does not equal Black lesbian woman: The methodological challenges of qualitative and quantitative intersectionality research. *Sex Roles, 59*, 312-325.

Brah, A., & Phoenix, A. (2004). Ain't I a Woman? Revisiting intersectionality. *Journal of International Women's Studies, 5*, 75-86.

Braun, V., & Clarke, V. (2006). Using thematic analysis in psychology. *Qualitative Research in Psychology, 3*, 77-101.

Close, H. (2007). The use of photography as a qualitative research tool. *Nurse Researcher, 15*(1), 27-36.

Cochran, S. D., & Mays, V. M. (1994). Depressive distress among homosexually active African American men and women. *American Journal of Psychiatry, 151*(4), 524-529.

Collier, J., & Collier, M. (1986). *Visual anthropology*. Albuquerque: University of New Mexico Press.

Collins, P. (1990). *Black feminist thought: Knowledge, consciousness, and the politics of empowerment*. London: Harper Collins Academic.

Hall, R. L., & Greene, B. (2002). Not any one thing: The complex legacy of social class on African American lesbians' relationships. *Journal of Lesbian Studies, 6*(1), 65-74.

Hariman, R., & Lucaites, J. (2003). Public identity and collective memory in U.S. iconic photography: The image of "Accidental Napalm." *Critical Studies in Media Communication*, 20, 35-66.

Harper, D. (1988). The visual ethnographic narrative. *Visual Anthropology*, 1(1), 1-19.

Howard, S. C. (2011). Breaking the silence: An autoethnography of a single, Black, lesbian's interpersonal relationships at an HBCU. In E. Gilchrist (Ed.), *Experiences of single African-American women professors: With this Ph.D., I thee wed* (pp. 159-174). Lanham, MD: Lexington.

Howard, S., & Lewis, M. (2011). African American lesbians watching "The L Word": Audience research. In T. Morrison, M. Morrison, M. Carrigan, & D. McDermott (Eds.), *Sexual minority research in the new millennium* (pp. 107-126). New York: Nova Science.

Lincoln, C. E., & Mamiya, L. H. (1990). *The Black church in the African American experience*. Durham, NC: Duke University Press.

Lorde, A. (1984). *Sister outsider*. New York: Crossing.

Mays, V. M., & Cochran, S. D. (1986). The Black women's relationship project: A national survey of Black lesbians. *Sourcebook*, 54-62.

McCall, L. (2005). The complexity of intersectionality. *Signs: Journal of Women in Culture and Society*, 30, 171-180.

Moore, M. (2006). Lipstick or Timberlands? Meanings of gender presentation in Black lesbian communities. *Signs: Journal of Women in Culture and Society*, 32, 114-139.

Pink, S. (2001). *Doing visual ethnography: Images, media and representation in research*. London: Sage.

Sampson-Cordle, A. (2001). Exploring the relationship between a small rural school in northeast Georgia and its community: An image based study using participant-produced photographs. PhD dissertation, University of Georgia. Abstract in *Dissertation Abstracts International*, 41, 411.

Samuels, J. (2004). Breaking the ethnographer's frames: Reflections on the use of photo elicitation in understanding Sri Lankan monastic culture. *American Behavioral Scientist*, 47(12), 1528-1550.

Shockley, A. (1983). The Black lesbian in American literature: An overview. In B. Smith (Ed.), *Home girls: a Black feminist anthology* (pp. 83-94). New York: Kitchen Table Women of Color.

Stephens, D., & Phillips, L. (2003). Freaks, gold diggers, divas, and dykes: The socio-historical development of African American adolescent women's sexual scripts. *Sexuality and Culture*, 7(1), 3-49.

Strickland, M., Keats, J., & Marinak, B. (2010).Connecting worlds: Using photo narrations to connect immigrant children, preschool teachers, and immigrant families. *School Community Journal*, 20, 81-102.

Sturken, M., & Cartwright, L. (2009). *Practices of looking: An introduction to visual culture*. New York: Oxford University Press.

Ulrike, B. (2002, July). Twenty years of public health research: Inclusion of lesbian, gay, bisexual, and transgender populations. *American Journal of Public Health*, 92(7), 1125-1130.

Wang, C. (1999). Photovoice: A participatory action research strategy applied to women's health. *Journal of Women's Health*, 8, 185-192.

Wang, C., & Burris, M. (1997). Photovoice: Concept, methodology, and use for participatory needs assessment. *Health Education and Behaviour*, 24, 369-387.

Wang, C., & Pies, C. A. (2004). Family, maternal, and child health through photovoice. *Maternal and Child Health Journal, 8*, 95–102.

Ward, E. G. (2005). Homophobia, hypermasculinity and the US black church. *Culture, Health & Sexuality, 7*(5), 493–504.

Warner, L. R. (2008). A best practices guide to intersectional approaches in psychological research. *Sex Roles, 59*, 454–463.

West, R., & Turner, L. H. (2010). *Introduction to communication theory: Analysis and application* (3rd ed.). Boston: McGraw-Hill.

Wood, J. T. (1994). *Who cares? Women, care, and culture.* Carbondale: Southern Illinois University Press.

CHAPTER 4

Black Queer Identity Matrix: Theoretical Framework

As discussed throughout this volume, we are in desperate need of paradigmatic inquiry around the intersections of gender, sexual orientation, and race/ethnicity. Current literature around queer studies does not adequately acknowledge the complexities of racial/ ethnic identity coupled with gender in expressing, negotiating, and constructing identity. Rather than an attempt to theorize the spectrum of racial minorities that also identify as lesbian, gay, bisexual, transgender, or questioning (LGBTQ) and hence speak for and about experiences of which I am not fully familiar, I will restrict my theorizing to Black lesbian women with the expectation that this framework may be heuristically adequate in expanding across Black queer identities and other racial minorities within the LGBTQ community.

The development of the Black Queer Identity Matrix is grounded in the work of scholars in the fields of anthropology, rhetoric, sociology, and communication. Such an acknowledgment is important in encouraging the reader to identify and understand how the Black Queer Identity Matrix described in this book is found largely within existing work in critical and interpretive theory. This chapter describes three specific theoretical frameworks—Afrocentricity, standpoint theory, and matrix of domination—that facilitated the development of a paradigm that addresses the communicative experiences of Black lesbian women within the structures of dominant society.

Across the next several pages, tenets of Nancy C. M. Hartsock's standpoint theory (1998), Molefi Asante's Afrocentricity (1988), and Patricia Hill Collins's (1986) matrix of domination will be revisited, in turn, as the platform to contextualizing the Black Queer Identity Matrix.

Introduction

Everyday people, not the elite, provide the framework for standpoint theory because of the belief that they possess knowledge different from that of those in power (West & Turner, 2010). As a minority on three counts—a Black lesbian female—my lived experiences are understood through the lens of a triple jeopardy minority. There are particular issues formed at the intersection of race, gender, and sexual orientation for a Black female lesbian (see Bowleg, 2008; Howard, 2011; Howard & Lewis, 2011), thus I interpret and conceptualize all material life through the lens of a triple jeopardy minority. This lens may not always be in direct opposition to those in power, but at minimum it is birthed from a unique social position. These unique social positions illuminate the need for a framework in which scholars can build on and actively seek the thoughts, interactions, and struggles of Black lesbian women. For example, the central concept of the theory, standpoint, is a location shared by a group experiencing outsider status within the social structure that lends a particular kind of sense making to a person's lived experiences.

The objectives of this work are twofold: (1) substantiate the need for an integrative conceptual framework around race, gender, and sexual orientation, especially from the position of a communication phenomena; and (2) show that the intersecting identities of race, gender, and sexual orientation are not experienced in isolation for Black lesbian women but that these identities act as interlocking systems of oppression.

This work is not making the argument that all Black lesbian women think, act, or look alike; however, by fusing Afrocentricity, standpoint theory, and the matrix of domination, I seek to acknowledge that this shared identity influences ontological and epistemological understandings of the world that are worthy of study through a framework that acknowledges the complexity of said identity. As a result, researchers can begin to seek out and examine the unique and distinct communication patterns, interests, perspectives, and experiences that shape the Black lesbian female community. Without this acknowledgment, researchers will continue to examine these identities in isolation, continue to ignore race and ethnicity under the umbrella of Judith Butler's queer theory when studying Black lesbian women, or continue to further marginalize the Black lesbian female community by not recognizing the unique social positions of this historically oppressed group.

The common outcome of conventional research is a propensity toward encouraging generalizations on the basis of scientific findings with representative samples of subjects. However, the line of scholarly research employed in the construction of the Black Queer Identity Matrix is grounded in a deliberate attempt to avoid such inclinations. As a result, the Black Queer Identity Matrix attempts to promote scholarship that acknowledges the specific case as much as the general tendency (see Orbe, 1998). For example, researchers in standpoint theory wish to begin with the marginalized and focus on their stories and interpretations (West & Turner, 2010). Thus, applying the tenets of standpoint theory is essential in promoting research on a small, yet significant, minority while harboring the ability to promote research on culture and communication.

Standpoint Theory

Standpoint theory explores the daily-life experiences of persons in subordinate positions. Rooted in Marxian analysis of working-class conditions (Hartsock, 1983), standpoint theory is grounded in recent work by Collins (1986, 2009), Nielsen (1990), and Smith (1987). Standpoint theory has traditionally been used as a feminist theoretical framework to explore the lived experiences of women as they participate in and oppose their own subordination (Hartsock, 1983), but applications of standpoint theory as it relates to other subordinate groups have been utilized as well (see Swignoski, 1994). Standpoint theory focuses on perspectives of women, but also could take the perspectives of African American women, poor White women/men, non-White women and men and individuals belonging to minority ethnic and religious groups outside modern Western society (see Orbe, 1998).

Fundamental Tenets of Standpoint Theory

Standpoint refers to a specific societal position, the result of one's field of experience, that serves as a subjective vantage point from which persons interact with themselves and the world (Orbe, 1998). A standpoint is not simply a subjective position that is interested in promoting bias but an acknowledgement of the sense of being engaged within a specific field of experience (Orbe).

Standpoint theory stands on the conviction that research must begin from one's concrete lived experiences rather than abstract concepts (Orbe, 1998). Therefore, that is why the Black Queer Identity Matrix was birthed out scholarship that seeks to explicate and understand the experiences of Black lesbian women through ethnographic and autoethnographic methods.

Standpoint theory rests on five specific assumptions about the nature of social life (West & Turner, 2010). These five assumptions will be discussed in turn. The first assumption is that "material life (or class position) structures and limits understandings of social relations" (West & Turner, p. 505). This assumption is particularly essential to the development of a more integrated queer of color framework such as the Black Queer Identity Matrix because it sets forth the notion that a person's location in the class structure shapes and limits his or her understanding of social relations (West & Turner, p. 505). The second assumption states, "When there is a dominant and subordinate group, the understanding of the dominant group will be both partial and harmful" (West & Turner, p. 506). Standpoint theory recognizes that no one has a complete view of social hierarchy and social status; however, those who are members of the nondominant group are more likely to be affected in a negative way by power structures because they do not hold the authority or dominance afforded to the dominant group. Black lesbian women, as minorities on three counts, do not hold economic, political, or social power, and thus they are likely to be disproportionally misrepresented, marginalized, and devalued, which is why it is imperative that we have a framework to address these dynamics.

Assumption three states, "The vision of the ruling group structures the material relations in which all groups are forced to participate" (West & Turner, 2010, p. 506). Hartsock (1997) comments that the "truth is, to a large extent, what the dominant groups can make true; history is always written by the winners" (p. 96). Thus, the choices and opportunities of the subordinate group are limited. For example, most people have very little choice about participating in a market economy that is the preferred mode for the ruling class (West & Turner, p. 506). These structures, which limit the choices of minorities, need to be further explored and explicated within the Black lesbian female community as very limited research has addressed these political and economic issues within the community. Hence, the Black Queer Identity Matrix offers a framework to address such forces.

Assumption four states, "The vision available to an oppressed group represents struggle and achievement" (West & Turner, 2010, p. 506). Consequently, subordinate groups have to struggle in order for their vision of social life to materialize. For example, lesbian women and gay men struggle for equal rights, such as marriage equality and equal employment opportunity rights. People of color have long fought for fair hiring practices and women continue to fight for equal pay and equal economic power, among other things. All of these seemingly basic rights are things that minority groups have to struggle and fight for in order for change to come. Thus, standpoints are positions that people take in direct opposition of those in power (or in direct opposition of the status quo). Last, assumption five states, "The potential understanding of the oppressed (the standpoint) makes visible the inhumanity of the existing relations among groups and moves us toward a better and more just world" (West & Turner, p. 506). This assumption is essential in moving toward an integrated queer of color framework as the ability for researchers to explore the standpoints of the Black lesbian community and the ways in which they view the system as oppressive and detrimental are invaluable in moving toward a more just world.

For the construction and explication of the Black Queer Identity Matrix, one added assumption must be noted. This assumption, which is characterized by Hartsock's Marxist view of standpoint theory posits that cultural conditions typically surrounding women's lives produce experiences and understandings that routinely differ from those produced by conditions framing men's lives (West & Turner, 2010). These different understandings often produce distinct communication patterns. These patterns are what the Black Queer Identity Matrix seeks to explicate. An example of these distinct communication patterns can be found in a study that examined sexual harassment and the workplace. It found that behaviors women found as harassing and dysfunctional were often perceived by men as ways of showing camaraderie and coping with a stressful work environment (Dougherty, 2001). Social and cultural conditions produce these different experiences and understandings.

Tenets of Afrocentricity as Vehicle

Afrocentric theoretical concepts are inherent to the explication and comprehension of the construction of the Black Queer Identity Matrix. Afrocentricity is a culture-centered framework that seeks to place African ideals at the center of phenomenon. According to Asante (2003):

> Afrocentricity is a mode of thought and action in which the centrality of African interests, values, and perspectives dominate. In regards to theory, it is the placing of African people in the center of any analysis of African phenomenon. Thus it is possible for anyone to master the discipline of seeking the location of African in a given phenomenon. In terms of action and behavior, it is a devotion to the idea that what is in the best interest of African consciousness is at the heart of ethical behavior. Finally, Afrocentricity seeks to enshrine the idea that blackness itself is a trope of ethics. Thus, to be Black is to be against all forms of oppression, racism, classism, homophobia, patriarchy, child abuse, pedophilia, and White racial domination. (p. 2)

Thus, essential to the construction of the Black Queer Identity Matrix is that Afrocentricity, as a culture-centered framework, is used as a means of analyzing cultural traditions as well as the communication traditions and practices carried over from Africa. Thus, the importance of grounding the Black Queer Identity Matrix in an Afrocentric perspective substantiates the importance of discovering the unique communicative practices and nuances within minority communities. For example, characteristics such as humanism, communalism, empathetic understanding, and rhythm, as well as the attributes of oppression-paranoia and the principle of limited reward, are foundational components of the African American communication process (Dixon & Foster cited in Asante, 1988). Accordingly, it is reasonable to believe that Black lesbian women engage in unique communication practices that need to be further examined.

Black lesbian women engage in a variety of communication strategies to challenge (and possibly reinforce) the status quo. In other words, they have embraced a cultural communication system in order to survive and succeed within the oppressive structures of dominant society, as seen in chapter 3. How do Black lesbian women manage? They communicate with other Black lesbian women for support, solidarity, motivation, and reassurance. They also employ various strategically positioned approaches in terms of artifacts that act as tools of empowerment, for example, wearing wife beaters in order to feel more powerful or in control. They establish a variety of communication strategies to gain their voices within and outside of dominant structures.

Afrocentric discourse represents discourse that seeks to bring about harmony and transcendence within and across the African American community. Operating from this standpoint, the marginalization of the LGBTQ community of color within the larger African American community poses an antagonistic opposition toward realizing said harmony or transcendence. Thus, homophobia within the African American community presents a hindrance to the impetus of collectivity and communalism so central to Afrocentricity. Thus, a queer of color framework needs to move scholars toward a more integrated analysis of the complexities of race, gender (and gender expression), and sexual orientation by taking cultural hegemony (culture specific power dynamics) into consideration as a significant variable as it relates to queer of color identity. Current frameworks such as but not limited to Judith Butler's queer theory egregiously ignores race, ethnicity, and culture, leaving any scholarship on the queer of color community void of comprehensive and critical analysis because an exploration of cultural essence is not possible. As such, a comprehensive framework is needed and this essay argues that Afrocentricity posits a practical starting place.

The theory of Afrocentricity involves placing African ideals at the center of any analysis that involves African culture and behavior (Asante, 1988, 1990). In *Kemet, Afrocentricity, and Knowledge* (1990), Asante expresses that the Afrocentrist "seeks to uncover and use codes, paradigms, symbols, motifs, myths, and circles of discussion that reinforce the centrality of African ideals and values as a valid frame of reference for acquiring and examining data" (p. 6). Afrocentricity does not seek to operate from an essentialist standpoint, thus it recognizes that differences exist between Africans throughout the world. Asante (2003) asserts that Africans in the United States, Costa Rica, Mexico, Jamaica, Haiti, Cuba, Puerto Rico, Barbados, Brazil, Venezuela, and beyond use diverse forms of the same African cultural system. The theory does not suggest that the African worldview is center for all people—just those of African descent. In fact, it encourages people to connect to the worldview most closely associated with their cultural heritage (Asante, 2003; Mazama, 2001). Thus, the Afrocentric perspective celebrates diversity within the language continuum by embracing pidgins, Creoles, and African American Vernacular English while also embracing new forms of communication characteristics throughout the African diaspora. This same diversity needs to be shared as it relates to sexuality within the African diaspora. The diversity of the African American community as well as African American history can serve as a catalyst to liberation if, and only if, the larger dominant heterosexual community is open to accepting its queer brothers and sisters—queer brothers and sisters that share some of the same cultural forms and struggles as the African American heterosexual community as well as the African diaspora.

It is not the position of this essay to posit that a queer of color framework needs to place African ideals at the center of each analysis; however, it is essential that the framework recognizes that there are common experiences and struggles affecting members of the Black queer community throughout the diaspora. As such, race, gender, and sexual orientation are not inseparable identities but identities that work together as interlocking systems of oppression within a White patriarchal society. Thus, though diverse in individual personalities, it is obvious that the Black queer community harbors shared experiences and a unique relationship to cultural norms as distinct from the White queer community.

This is not "blacker-than-thou" rhetoric as Gregory Conerly in Queer Studies suggests; it is the recognition that an integrated Black queer of color theory, such as the framework proposed in this essay, does not need to establish guidelines of Blackness. It does, however, need to acknowledge that the Black queer community experience is distinct, and it shares in unique experiences that their White LGBTQ counterparts do not and will never experience, as such gender adds to this unique experience.

Race, Gender, and Sexual Orientation as Interlocking Systems of Oppression

Race, class, and gender create a matrix of domination that women of color experience—and resist—on three levels, namely the level of personal biography; the group level of the cultural context created by race, class, and gender; and the systemic level of social institutions (Collins, 1986).

Moreover, Patricia Hill Collins writes about the matrix of domination in her book *Black Feminist Thought* (2009). In it she states, "The matrix of domination refers to how intersecting oppressions are actually organized" (p. 21). The matrix of domination allows researchers to critique how systems of power, domination, and oppression are produced, reproduced, and constrained (Collins, 2009). However, Collins's matrix of domination is not sympathetic to the specific construct of sexual orientation or the dialectical tension of race and gender for the Black lesbian female.

Gay men find themselves within a matrix of domination because of the notion of Black masculinity and what it means to be a Black male. Collins's (1986) framework is not inclusive of the intersections of race, gender, and specifically sexual orientation as it relates to men and women of color. Being gay is antithetical to the common understanding of Black masculinity as strong, domineering, emotionless, breadwinners, and hypersexual (see Majors & Billson, 1992; Jackson, 2006). The notion of masculinity has for a very long time been tied to sources of homophobia and heterosexuality. According to some scholars, this is especially true for Black communities (see Boykin, 1996). Consequently, gay men struggle with the constraints of social structures on three levels as well. Thus, members of the Black queer community are working within a Black Queer Identity Matrix. In addition, undoubtedly communication tools are used to cope and survive in the face of these structures or within this matrix.

The Black Queer Identity Matrix proposed in this book allows for a combination of intersectionality and the matrix of domination by providing an agenda for understanding how race, gender, and sexual orientation intersect in the lives of not only Black lesbian women but possibly Black gay men as well (although not the main focus of this book). The framework also allows for the deconstruction of the larger dominate community in general. For example, the African American community is unique in that it is a minority group that is said to be extremely homophobic, which undermines harmonic progress for the Black LGBTQ community. This may seem surprising as the African American community is also known as a minority that has struggled for equality, justice, and acceptance within American society; as such, struggle must sit at the centerpiece of a Black queer conceptual framework.

Implications of the Black Queer Identity Matrix

This chapter will end by proposing a conceptual framework that seeks to reiterate the deficiencies of queer theory for the Black lesbian female and create an amalgamation of standpoint theory, matrix of domination, and Afrocentricity as vehicles toward creating a more integrated conceptual framework for Black female lesbians of color called the Black Queer Identity Matrix. Tenets of standpoint theory (Nancy C. M. Hartsock), the matrix of domination (Patricia Hill Collins), and Afrocentricity (Molefi Asante) can provide the starting point for conceptualization around a framework that seeks to illuminate the complexities of the Black female lesbian identity.

Standpoint theory focuses on sex and gender as opposed to sexual orientation, thus the power structures at work in one's social life—as it relates to race, gender, and sexual orientation—of Black lesbian women are not fully encompassed within this theoretical framework. An integrated framework that revolves around Black female sexuality will come about as more research is produced around the Black lesbian community. Thus, the Black Queer Identity Matrix can be used in order to examine the multiple intersecting identities of this population.

The matrix of domination allows researchers to critique how systems of power, domination, and oppression are produced, reproduced, and constrained (Collins, 2009). However, Patricia Hill Collins's matrix of domination is not sympathetic to the specific construct of sexual orientation or the dialectical tension of race and gender for the Black lesbian female. Collins's work makes it abundantly clear that oppressed identities work together and create a lens through which individuals experience the world, which makes it all the more vital to examine the interlocking systems of oppression and the materialization of this particular oppression within the Black lesbian community. Currently, scholars do not have a framework to do this.

An Afrocentric perspective seeks to move toward a much needed transcendence and harmony within the African American community. The aforementioned notion is integral to the development of a new framework seeking to bridge the gap between the dominant heterosexual community and the queer of color community; a divided community cannot realize harmony and transcendence. Thus, a viable Black queer framework needs to recognize the struggles and oppression of African Americans while seeking the unity of the community in order to elucidate the multiple intersecting identities of said community—the Black Queer Identity Matrix. For example, a Black queer conceptual framework can be used as an umbrella to address the unique cultural variables that influence the "coming out"¹ process across the queer of color community as a distinctive process understood from a cultural perspective as opposed to a Eurocentric perspective.

A Black queer theoretical framework is needed to address and redress the divisiveness of the Black community along the lines of sexual orientation. The Black female lesbian finds herself in a matrix of interlocking systems of oppression that pivots around negotiating and communicating sexual identity when navigating within the dominant society as well as her own Black community. These complexities need to be further examined by researchers in order to understand the location or standpoint "shared by a group experiencing outsider status, within the social structure" (West & Turner, 2010, p. 508).

The Black Queer Identity Matrix proposed in this work acknowledges the variables of race and ethnicity as well as sexual identity and gender. It seeks to explore the unique strategies employed by the Black queer community in order to better understand this understudied population as well as encourage discussion around the unique challenges of this complex identity.

Integral Assumptions to Consider

After reviewing the existing interdisciplinary literatures and conceptualizations of Black female lesbian identity, as well as the overarching umbrella of Black queer identity, it is clear that a Black queer conceptual framework needs to operate and be founded from a set of assumptions that speak to the interlocking identities of race, gender (as well as gender expression), and sexual orientation. The following assumptions are based on thematic patterns in the literature on Black female sexuality (see Collins, 2009; Bobo, 1995; Bowleg, 2008; Howard, 2011) and on the pilot study I conducted on Black lesbian female identity (see chapter 3). This study confirms what much of the current literature states about "double" and "triple" minorities: that individuals operating from multiple oppressed identities should not be forced to disaggregate identities. It also identifies coping mechanisms employed by Black lesbian females as they navigate the world.

This work offers the following as assumptions, based on literature review and theoretical considerations throughout this volume, to consider as scholarship moves toward a more integrated Black queer conceptual framework:

1. Sexual orientation and race exist primarily as social constructs.
2. Struggle is the centerpiece of a Black queer conceptual framework because of the history of oppression within the Black community.
3. Race, gender (as well as gender expression), and sexual orientation are interlocking systems of oppression.
4. Different social locations and social knowledges often produce distinct communication patterns.
5. The Black lesbian female experience can be known only by attending to Black lesbian female interpretations of this experience.

Due to the various forms of discrimination weighted on the triple minority identity of the Black lesbian female, researchers should explore the various communication and coping mechanisms employed by this community. The amalgamation of intersectionality impregnated by the Black lesbian female identity is the core of the Black Queer Identity Matrix.

The experiences of Black lesbian women and communication are reciprocal in nature, for communication is used to both shape and transmit one's social knowledge and social position. Communication is responsible for shaping our identity because we learn our place in society as a result of our interactions with others. In addition, Black lesbian women sharing a similar identity often adopt similar communication styles and practices as they navigate and learn to survive within a dominant and oppressive system. Research by Stanback and Pearce (1981) approaches the study of marginalized groups with the recognition that these persons must somehow operate within the constraints imposed by their self-concepts, intentions, and an awareness of dominant group expectations. Therefore, research that links the communicative experiences of different marginalized groups is important. Mark Orbe, in *Constructing Co-cultural Theory* (1998), states:

> Exploring the various ways in which those without societal power devise communication tactics when communicating with those with power is a valuable point of examination for communication researchers. Beyond providing an intersection for scholarly inquiry related to culture, power, and communication, it also represents a celebration of human creativity. Second, analysis of common strategies used by those marginalized by dominant society informs the development of human communication theory. (p. 31)

Critique

There is one critique that I want to address as this framework is sure to be attacked along the lines of essentialism. Thus, one of the easiest critiques of this framework, as well as any framework that is centered on a particular minority group, is that it is essentialist. The Black Queer Identity Matrix is not to say that Black lesbian women are not varied or that they all share the same attitudes, values, and beliefs. However, this is to say that Black lesbian women as a collective have experiences and struggles in which they can relate that create distinctive communication patterns worth investigating. In short, if someone can name one culture-centered framework that has not been criticized along the lines of essentialism, I would be surprised.

The Black Queer Identity Matrix theoretical framework is a humanistic theory, thus it has several strong points. Nevertheless, the theory as it stands in present form does have some limitations. This is largely due to the fact that the Black Queer Identity Matrix is in its infancy form and the hope is that scholars apply the framework within their own scholarship so that the ideas can be furthered explicated and explored.

A "matrix" is an environment or material in which something develops. According to Merriam-Webster's (2012) online dictionary, a matrix is a material in which something is enclosed or embedded; thus, Black lesbians are members within an environment that has the power to shape one's sense of self and to rearrange or challenge one's own worldview. Black lesbian women are a product of all the nuances of the United States—social hierarchy, capitalism, sexism, racism, heterosexism, a market economy, neoliberalism, to name a few—that influences one's communication patterns as well as one's own self-awareness. Therefore, Black lesbian women are enclosed or embedded within the fabric of America and must survive despite inequality and oppressive structural systems. There is a lot to learn from this small, yet vital, segment of society, especially as the gay rights movement progresses and as the visibility of the LGBTQ community increases.

The Black Queer Identity Matrix at Work

In this section, I reflect from both an intellectual and personal standpoint on historically based constructions of Black gender expression and the implications of those constructions through the lens of the Black Queer Identity Matrix. The ethnographic and autoethnographic work I have done around Black lesbian identity (including the work in this volume) largely informs the following discussion on Black lesbian gender expression.

In studying the Black lesbian community, as a participant in the community and an academic researcher, I have observed characteristics of the community along the lines of gender presentation and romantic interpersonal relationships that, I argue, are symptoms of White patriarchy and Black hegemonic masculinity, which the Black Queer Identity Matrix seeks to extrapolate. The LGBTQ community still exists within a larger dominant ideology that influences the intricacies of various communities within the gay-lesbian community, including the Black lesbian community. This is not to suggest that similar dynamics are not readily apparent in other LGBTQ communities; however, there is undoubtedly a masculine-feminine dynamic that is pervasive in the Black lesbian community—specifically in Black lesbian relationships—which has historical, social, and cultural underpinnings that need to be unpacked. Thus, the Black Queer Identity Matrix allows us to focus on cultural underpinnings of the Black lesbian community and ascertain the ways in which a people's history and worldview influence communication patterns, both verbal and nonverbal, of the members within the community. This is also not to suggest that the entirety of the Black lesbian community is monolithic in its thinking and experiences. However, I am here to unpack phenomena within and across the Black lesbian community so as to encourage discussion around the intricacies of the Black lesbian community.

As the Black Queer Identity Matrix posits, the continuity and extension of American history and African American history influences the state of the community today. Thus, I begin this discussion by reviewing the literature around Black masculinity, and then I make the connection between Black masculinity and the implications for Black lesbian gender expression and interpersonal relationships.

Understanding terminology frequently used in the Black lesbian community is vital to the comprehension of this work. Therefore, I will offer an operational definition of "studs" and "femmes" for the mere purposes of describing, defining, and theorizing about Black lesbian identity.

A "stud" is a lesbian woman (a term predominantly used in the Black lesbian community) who dresses and acts in ways comparable to Black men. They dress in ways that are comparable to their Black male peers: baggy pants and shirts, hats, high-top shoes, Timberland boots, and fairly flashy jewelry are common (Lane-Steele, 2011). As discussed early on in this text, the historical foundations of this identity have been connected to the feminist movement as Black women were excluded from participating in it; therefore, they were never fully liberated from the rigid binaries of gender presentation. Mignon Moore (2006) states:

> After the 1960s, the association between lesbian identity and the women's liberation movement intersected so much that lesbian-feminist perspectives on gay identity began to overshadow the experiences of lesbians who were unconnected to that movement, gay women whose lives were being shaped by other events in their social worlds. Black women-identified women were one group of lesbians who were never fully indoctrinated into the particular type of feminism espoused during the 1960s and 1970s. (p. 115)

Moore continues, "Since many black women were never fully part of white lesbian-feminist leadership or on board with all of its goals, they were less influenced by efforts to replace butch and femme identities with androgynous presentations of self" (p. 117).

A stud identity often includes a female who considers herself to have a more dominant personality in regard to romantic relationships and usually will only date a "femme." Femmes are lesbian women in the Black lesbian community who typically dress more feminine and are, theoretically, more submissive within the context of romantic relationships.

> These stud-femme relationships follow many of the same scripts of normative Black heterosexual couples their age. Studs call themselves the "boy" of the relationship. They pay for dates and are expected to be dominant over and in control of their girlfriends. Many of them use extremely misogynist language, referring to their girlfriend as "my bitch" or "my ho," and saying things like "Man, that bitch thinks I love her, but I just like to fuck her." (Lane-Steele, 2011, p. 486)

In essence, there is a trending phenomenon within the Black lesbian community in which romantic relationships tend to mirror heterosexual relationships in which there is a masculine and feminine dichotomy reflective of heteronormativity. It is my position that these dynamics need to be further deconstructed through the lens of the Black Queer Identity Matrix—which allows for the study of cultural elements within the African American community to be included in any analysis of the Black lesbian community; that is what the following pages seek to do.

Before moving forward, I want to acknowledge (as the Black Queer Identity Matrix acknowledges) that there are varied gender expressions within the Black lesbian community and not all studs or femmes conform to the previously described characteristics. In addition, there are gender expressions that fall on a broad spectrum ranging from stud to femme and everything in between. However, the purpose of this discussion is to analyze the stud-femme dichotomy, with specific attention to the social, cultural, and historical underpinnings of the stud identity based on racial and gendered historical constructions within and across the African American community.

With that being said, I want to start by emphasizing that if we, that is, members of the LGBTQ community, continue to say "studs dress masculine" or "studs look like men," then we will never truly be liberated as far as gender expression is concerned because we will, through language, view a certain style of clothing as masculine or that of something a man would wear. Thus, we are contributing to marginalization and oppression of lesbian gender expression. True liberation is to move toward the point in which clothing is not categorized as masculine or feminine but simply a preference of what one desires to wear. To break free from labels, we first have to break free from the language that gives life and shape to those labels. The lesbian community can further challenge the status quo by rejecting the use of terms such as "masculine" and "feminine" to describe varied gender expression. In reality, studs challenge the hegemonic idea that biological maleness is necessary for masculinity (Halberstam, 1998). Female masculinity embodied by these studs proves that biological sex is not a determinant or a requirement of gender expression (Lane-Steele, 2011).

Black Masculinity: A Review

Like all gender performances, the stud personification is constructed from cultural norms or speaking back to cultural norms within a society; in this case the construction of a stud identity is constructed through the exemplification of Black masculinity. The matrix in which we live shapes our identity, way of life and worldview. The stud identity does not exist in isolation of ones environment, but instead it is a performed gender constructed from taking cues (clothes, mannerisms, style of speech, gestures, etc.) from ones surroundings and embodying those cues. As such, the Black Queer Identity Matrix posits that race and sexual orientation are merely social constructions. In essence, this performativity of gender forms and informs ones notions of identity. The following is a brief review of the literature surrounding Black masculinity and the construction of Black male identity (Lane-Steele, 2011, p. 485). This will lead the discussion toward Black lesbian studs and the implications of Black masculinity as studs emulate the characteristics and mannerisms of their Black male peers.

Numerous studies have shown the importance of economic, interpersonal, and sociohistorical influences on how African American men learn to conceptualize their masculine identities (Roberts-Douglass & Curtis-Boles, 2012).

Majors and Billson (1992), in particular, address the compensatory strategies and mechanisms performed and embodied by Black males in order to cope with racial oppression. African American men have long compensated for feelings of inadequacy or inability to meet the Eurocentric standards of gender roles. Harris (1995) indicates that physical posture, speech, walking style, form of greeting, and style of clothing function as mannerisms consistent with alternative masculinity for African American men.

Majors and Billson (1992), and Collins (2009) have discussed how hypermasculinity constructs as a kind of "strong Black man," "cool pose," and "real man" demeanor among Black men (Oware, 2010). Roberts-Douglass and Curtis-Boles (2012) further suggest:

> To compensate for such feelings, African American males have redefined masculinity to highlight and value attributes such as toughness and sexual promiscuity. In addition, Harris indicates that physical posture, speech, walking style, form of greeting, and style of clothing function as mannerisms consistent with alternative masculinity for African American men. Furthermore, these behaviors include suppression of emotions, denial of vulnerability, and a predominant heterosexual focus. These characteristics are consistent with Major's (1989) definition of "cool pose," which refers to African American males' reliance on hypermasculine "roles, values, and presentation of self" to deal with stressful conditions. (p. 8)

According to Majors and Billson (1992), "Of all the strategies embraced by black males to cope with oppression and marginality, the creation of the cool pose is perhaps the most unique. Presenting to the world an emotionless, fearless, and aloof front counters the low sense of inner control, lack of inner strength, absence of stability, damaged pride, shattered confidence and fragile social competence that come from living on the edge of society" (p. 8).

African American men have long struggled to meet the traditional gender roles set forth by White America—provider, breadwinner, procreator, and protector. Historically, Black men have not been afforded the necessary resources to fulfill those roles. Neal (2006) claims its genesis began 400 years ago due to the enslavement, violence, and continued economic exploitation of this group. As a result, Black males created a "functional myth" to help them handle their plight (p. 21).

Since the days of slavery, African Americans have used coolness to express themselves without risking punishment (Majors & Billson, 1992). Thus, playing it cool becomes a vital element of Black manhood. Rather than reveal true feelings, Black men present a serene exterior in a brave attempt to project a composed, controlled self-image (Majors & Billson). Coolness becomes ritualized for the Black male, influencing not only his social persona but his intimate relationships as well. Cool behaviors may prevent Black males from developing authentic relationships with women (Majors & Billson). Thus, the behaviors that act as coping mechanisms for Black men in their daily lives are the same behaviors that inhibit successful relationships with women. There is a deeper level of complexity here as Black women often are attracted to Black men who act cool or look cool. Black women reward coolness. Majors and Billson (1992) suggest:

> Some women are attracted to the urbane, emotionless, smooth, fearless, aloof, apparently masculine qualities of the cool pose. The cool man is an enigma—a challenge to females. Comments, such as the following, express the black females' ambivalence toward cool pose: "I just don't know where he's coming from"; "He's just too cool." (p. 43)

Furthermore, Black males do not respect other Black males who do not display a strong image (Majors & Billson, 1992). Coinciding with the sociohistorical relationship between Black men and the construction of Black masculinity, the media play a vital role in commodifying Black male identity. The Black male image is a commodity and gangsta rap has created a hypermasculine archetype of what it means to be a Black man. Misogyny and female sexual objectification are staples around the performances of Black masculinity in rap music. The media perpetuate Black hegemonic masculinity or limited inscriptions of other ways to be masculine. This commodification of Black masculinity is a symptom of White patriarchy. However, the implications of Black hegemonic masculinity are not limited to Black heterosexual men and their interpersonal relationships, as the Black lesbian community also suffers from the inscriptions of Black masculinity as defined by a racist, patriarchal social system.

The music industry and the supplemental music videos are a powerful source for representing identities and current issues facing society. People often turn to music to express, to understand, or to celebrate their lives and culture. The growth in popularity and the commercial success of rap music emphasizes its social acceptance and cultural legitimization. A paradox exists between the constructed self and the commodification of the artist by the music producer. To be certain, the origins of rap music, and hip-hop culture more largely, must be situated within broader systemic processes of economic changes and federal policies. Rose argues, "Hip hop culture emerged as a source for youth of alternative identity formation and social status in a community whose older local support institutions had been all but demolished" (as cited in Pemberton, 2008, pp. 32-33). This speaks to the large response of systematic oppression and silencing of Black America by White supremacy. Black protest literature of the 1940s was dominated by the invisibility and silencing of Black males. This was met in the 1960s and 1970s with "the imagery and activity of strong Black warriors, frequently assumed to be male warriors" (Ross, 1998, p. 604).

The image of the real Black man developed and perpetuated in rap music would not exist without, according to Rux, "a historical narrative of, or opposes the construct of, these identities" (2003, p. 18). This idea is situated in and is a response to the colonial efforts and oppressive practices of the White man. The ideal form of masculinity has become known as hegemonic masculinity. This is illustrated by maintaining control and independence and a strictly compulsory heterosexuality. Any description counter to this notion of identity is a challenge to masculinity (e.g., lyrical content of or including images of emasculating men, not being tough enough, or homosexuality). Because of the realities of being Black men in the United States and these culturally perpetuated images, Black male hip-hop artists conform to the ideals of hegemonic masculinity (Rux, p. 10).

While gender, sexuality, and media scholars continue to deconstruct the representation and production of hypermasculinity in the media, and more directly the music industry, one could understand the excessive displays of heterosexuality and homophobia as a facade for male masculinity. In many ways, the use of barely clothed women who are overly sexualized and available to the male gaze in music videos and lyrics are the result of society's patriarchy, mediums of misogyny, and heteronormativity. The excessive signals and images of the masculine heterosexual are nonetheless expressions of what they believe a man or male is to be in current day America. Or, at the very least, they are reproduced fantasies that continue to normalize gender and sex/ual behaviors and acts. However, if we are to be honest with ourselves, we understand that to a large degree gender and sex/uality norms are taught and learned. While scholars and activists critique hip-hop images, messages, and the damaging effects they perpetuate with women and nonnormative genders, we understand that this process starts from birth—some might even say, prebirth. These constructions go unchallenged and contribute to the current day man and woman. By our teenage and young adult years, gender and sexuality roles have been strictly dictated and enforced by what we recognize sexism, heterosexism, and homonormativity to be.

To complicate this further, one can ask, what does it mean to be a Black man in America? What does it mean to be part of a Black diasporic cultural community? In the documentary *Hip-Hop: Beyond Beats and Rhymes* (2006), director and producer Byron Hurt suggests that homophobia, sexism, misogyny, and other forms of policing masculinity comes from a lack of knowing themselves. Men are afraid of embracing their femininity and sensitivity because, somehow, it makes them less than respectable. However, Hurt's point is to say that showing your emotion does not weaken you; rather, it strengthens you. That being said, the question remains how to get to know oneself as a Black man? What do you need to get in touch with? How can one challenge himself to become a Black man comfortably?

This "rebel" image of men and hip-hop artists originated as a mixed response to violence, systematic oppression, and the silencing of their families and neighborhoods. In an American history where the Black man stood as an object of inheritance to White slave owners, the current persona of a Black hip-hop artist can be read as a response to redeem his self and ego by overcompensating the "I" and "me" form of being. The supersized ego and material wealth is one theme running throughout hip-hop and portrays a narrow image of what a man and, more largely, a human means. This dual and semi-fantasy role the hip-hop artist takes on is a hybrid nature of proving oneself in a system that never meant for the Black male to succeed or account for anything, mixed with a capital agenda of selling the "life" with materialism and women. The danger in this fantasy world is that it carries real-life results. The images are not just about fun, games, and entertainment, they carry power and account for real effects. Mainstream hip-hop is not based in reality, the artists are playing and capitalizing on a fantasy world.

Mainstream hip-hop continues to be referred to and highly influenced by corporate White America. Without any doubt, young artists are under intense pressure to be controlled and perform "Blackness" to please mainstream market value, not the art itself. For example, Dr. Tricia Rose has talked extensively on the insertion of capitalism and violence against Black people and women in hip-hop. That being said, hip-hop is not responsible for sexism, homophobia, or misogyny, but it does participate in those systems because it reproduces and mimics society as a whole. It would also be an injustice not to examine how corporate America and capitalism profits off Black hypermasculinity and hyperaggression. The fighting, violence, and disposal of Black bodies feed White supremacy in all areas of economics, politics, and social discourses.

Professor Griff and Chuck D from the group Public Enemy have publicly stated that hip-hop needs to start loving women and put them back on the throne where their voices can be heard. They have also admitted to there being too much testosterone and hypermasculinity in the industry today. When dealing with the real-life experiences of misogyny and homophobia, we have to continue to educate men on violence against women and debunking what a "real man" means in the context of social justice.

The constructed masculine identities of rappers and hip-hop performance artists are often characterized as aggressive, violent, and arrogant. Butler (1990) claims, "The acts by which gender is constituted bear similarities to performative acts within theatrical contexts" (p. 272). Balaji (2009) poses the questions, "Do Black male performers have ownership over how their masculinity is depicted in music videos? If so, do these images conform to their sense of self or are they corporate constructions designed to sell the artist as a commodity?" (p. 22). More recent, there has been a push by many Black independent artists to reclaim their owning and producing rights in attempt to detach themselves from White mainstream corporations that have controlled their Black hip-hop artists via mechanisms like racial interpellation. In addition, in regards to identity and performativity, Nichols (2006) argues, "Neither identity can be viewed as real or fake" (p. 3). This existence of dual identifications is often overlooked but never the less holds valuable knowledge and experiences that dare to be explored.

Current mainstream discourses on hip-hop often blame rap and the industry for a range of highly offensive images and messages today's youth listen to but rarely do they focus on the positive sides. At a foundational level, music holds the ability to connect, heal, and educate. Hip-hop has been used as a form of expression, a survival mechanism, and storytelling specific to communities of color. However, that storytelling mechanism needs to be told by and for Black people; they need to be in charge of their own voices and oral tradition. Furthermore, hip-hop serves as a voice to the voiceless and is there to further consciousness, critical thinking, and thought. It is not singular but instead multimodal and global. The hip-hop movement continues to demonstrate the ability to inspire and change societies and cultures throughout the world. It is a call to revolutionize and reclaim our minds, bodies, and words.

This review of literature around Black masculinity was necessary in order to make connections among sexism, White patriarchy, and the Black lesbian community. From here on out, I will make the connection between male dominance and the influence on sexism within the lesbian community, as well as Black masculinity and its relationship to Black lesbian gender expression.

Black Lesbian Relationships and Internalized Sexism

Within the Black lesbian community the stud-femme dichotomy is a particular phenomenon in which lesbian relationships subscribe to a binary of one feminine partner and one masculine partner (see Lane-Steele, 2011; Moore, 2006; Wilson, 2009). Much of the time, feminine women exclusively prefer to date more masculine identified women and vice versa. I realize the contradiction in the aforementioned statement as I began this chapter with stating that we need to move away from referring to women as dressing "masculine" or "like a man"; however, for the purposes of articulating my argument and for lack of language alternatives, I rely on using familiar terminology within the remainder of this chapter in order to state clearly my position. I will leave it up to the reader to liberate the community and create alternative language tools as it relates to referring to unconventional modes of gender expression outside of the usage of the term "masculine."

According to Wilson (2009), "Within lesbian sexual culture, gendered sexual discourses have illuminated the myriad ways that lesbian women have used and expected one another to identify" (pp. 298-299). Gayle Rubin (1992) describes butch and femme as "ways of coding identities and behaviors that are both connected to and distinct from standard societal roles for men and women" (p. 467). Some scholars (Moore, 2006; Taylor & Rupp, 1993) argue that, historically, feminism was exclusive of women of color, including lesbian women of color, thus lesbians of color have not been historically liberated as it relates to gender expression. In Wilson's (2009) article "Black Lesbian Gender and Sexual Culture: Celebration and Resistance," the author states:

> One of the most significant forms of US second-wave feminist ritual that have characterized contemporary lesbian culture is the androgynous or "neither masculine nor feminine" mode of self-presentation. These ways of dressing and behaving have been presented as an oppositional stance against the mainstream dominant view of appropriate feminine expression. However, women of color and working class women have also asserted that these androgynous modes of expression are a cultural artifact of White middle class lesbians, not necessarily all lesbians. (p. 299)

The aforementioned accounts have been solidified by Audre Lorde's writings, among other Black feminists, during the early and mid-1990s. This resistance and struggle is a centerpiece of the Black Queer Identity Matrix as Black women and men have a history of oppression.

Audre Lorde spent much of her life challenging underlying racism within feminism. Much of Lorde's work compares racism within feminism as symptoms of White male patriarchy. Many feminists were outraged at Lorde's accusations and claimed that her intent was to privilege Black lesbian or Black female identity. As we look at the butch-femme dichotomy, which is so prevalent in the Black lesbian community, it becomes clear that the lack of inclusion of Black women in first- and second-wave feminism had and continues to have a profound effect on gender expression within and across the Black lesbian community.

> An in-depth qualitative study by Mignon Moore (2006) identified three categorizations of gender among Black lesbians, including femme, transgressive and

gender blender. Transgressive referred to more masculine-identified women, including masculine-identified women who did not like the terms butch and stud, whereas gender-blender referred to the mixing of explicitly feminine and masculine characteristics. Moore's study was an important step in the direction of documenting an often-ignored segment of US culture, Black lesbians. (Wilson, 2009, p. 300)

In Wilson's study of gender presentation within the Black lesbian community, she notes that Black lesbian women consistently used the term "stud" to identify or self-identify women who displayed a more masculine gender presentation.

Participants consistently highlighted lesbian gender roles as a key organizing construct of African American lesbian sexual life. Four participants claimed these labels for themselves. Several other participants supported women's adoption of these roles. The ways in which participants spoke about stud and femme categories indicated that these ways of constructing lesbian gender were part of an overarching sexual cultural norm of which all were aware. (p. 303)

Wilson further notes that Black lesbian women are almost expected to adopt a label and that the stud-femme dichotomy creates a "sexual script" for members of the Black lesbian community, both in romantic relationships and social settings. In addition she notes that the Black lesbian community often ostracizes couples who break the usual "gender" roles of stud or femme:

One masculine-masculine couple appeared to be participating in this type of transgression. Recognizing the discrepancy between their coupling and the cultural sexual scripts expectations, I asked that couple that night whether they had experienced negative reactions to their being a couple in which both women appeared masculine identified. They explained that they had received harsh reactions and lack of understanding from other African American lesbians. However, they felt that they were no longer into labels and loved each other. They had been together for over eight years and people knew them as an established couple so left them alone. (p. 304)

Within the Black lesbian community those who identify as stud or butch often times demand that they not be touched during sexual intercourse. In short, studs provide their femme partner with sexual pleasure but it cannot be returned.

One explanation was that hard studs were not comfortable with the parts of their bodies that defined them as female, mainly their breasts and vaginas. As such, a successful performance of the "male" role during sex required that the hard stud's female body parts not be touched. Another reason concerned the meaning of being touched and seduced. That is, participants talked about the importance of maintaining the appearance of dominance in the sexual act for hard studs and how being touched sexually or being the "bottom" took away that sense of dominance and control. (p. 305)

Though Wilson's study did a good job describing the gender roles prevalent within and across the Black lesbian community, the study did not assess the constructs and implications of the stud-femme dichotomy as it relates to the larger dominant cultural system within the United States.

As a member of the in-group, the implications are as follows: It is frowned upon for stud women to date other stud women (or two women whose gender presentation is more masculine). Interestingly enough, feminine women who partner with other feminine women are not largely frowned upon in the same way stud-on-stud relationships are. Therefore, the lesbian community itself is not a safe place for gender expression and fluid sexuality. Thus, as the Black Queer Identity Matrix posits in chapter 3, the Black lesbian female finds herself in a matrix of interlocking systems of oppression that pivots around negotiating and communicating sexual identity as well as navigating within the dominant society and her own Black community. The Black lesbian community does not allow studs, in particular, to convey a full range of sexual expression because the community at large is hindered by ideas of what is considered "normal," and stud-on-stud action is not considered normal within the Black lesbian community. In addition, feminine women have an expectation when dating studs that their personalities or innate characteristics will reflect that of a more masculine nature. Thus, studs or butch women are supposed to be more authoritative, less emotional, and exude the persona of the protector as well as be sexually dominant in the bedroom. In essence, these categories and labels associated with an individual simply predicated on her style of dress is oppressive. This oppression is a symptom of internalized sexism and internalized oppression from the dominance of male ideology. More specifically, the more feminine form of gender expression or the visual of two feminine women together is more acceptable or natural because of the ways in which we are socialized to view things from a male perspective. Through this view, we can see that women are being identified by physical appearance rather than based on their observable behaviors or relationships. Oppression targets individuals insofar as they are considered to be members of targeted groups, though individual group members differ in their exposure to oppression and their strategies for responding to it (Hill & Thomas, 2000; Swim & Hyers, 1999). The lack of liberation and freedom of sexual expression within the Black lesbian community is a symptom of the lack of inclusion within the feminist movement, as previously stated, and the internalization of sexist attitudes within the psyche of women. According to Bearman, Korobov, and Thorne (2009):

> Internalized sexism is not merely sexism perpetrated by women upon women. Sexism involves two distinct groups, one of which is systematically denied power by the other.

> In contrast, internalized sexism involves the internal dynamics within an oppressed group. It helps to maintain sexism as a whole via a system of social expectations and pressures enacted between women. (p. 14)

In order for sexism to exist, it must be practiced, and so it may be productive to consider internalized sexism to be a set of practices (Gutiérrez & Rogoff, 2003). These practices vary from one cultural context to another and are not universal or essential to gender (see Bearman, Korobov, & Thorne, 2009). Within this particular context sexism exists within the cultural setting of the Black lesbian community as it relates to gender expression and acceptance. In essence, there is a perceived prejudice against masculine-identified women who date other masculine-identified women, and masculine-identified women who do not live up to the expectations of what a stud ought to act like, both inside and outside of the bedroom. In short, men are not attracted to masculine-identified women and this ideology spills over into the psyche of expression and acceptance within the lesbian community. Bearman and colleagues state:

> In their self-objectification theory, Frederickson and Roberts (1997; Fredrickson, Roberts, Noll, Quinn, & Twenge, 1998; Hebl, King, & Lin, 2004) describe the process by which external experiences of objectification can become internalized. Due to the omnipresence of media images of women, and through the direct gazes of men, women are immersed in social environments in which they and other women are regularly looked at, evaluated on the basis of their appearance, and treated as if their bodies and looks represent something essential about their personhood. (p. 16)

Consequently, when we ponder why stud-on-stud relationships are frowned upon one does not have to look any further than Frederickson and Roberts self-objectification theory as "under these conditions, girls and women quickly learn the social importance of physical appearance and furthermore learn to adopt the stance of an outside observer in understanding their own bodies (Bearman et al., 2009, p. 17). The outside (sexist) observer becomes internalized, and women may come to experience their bodies primarily as they are seen from the outside and compared against external standards rather than as they are felt and inhabited from within (Tolman & Porche, 2000). This is precisely what is happening within the Black lesbian community. As romantic relationships seek to re-create normal gender identities of a masculine and feminine role, a relationship consisting of two masculine-identified women further challenges what is considered normal within a relationship; and it is not appealing thru the male gaze, which is a symptom of comparing lesbian relationships against external standards—the standards of the male perspective.

Men enjoy seeing two feminine women together but are less likely to want to see two masculine-identified women together. Thus, members of the lesbian community are not immune to the socialization and influence of the male gaze and, in return, internalize this destructive and oppressive way of viewing romantic relationships within and across the Black lesbian community. One has to question the larger societal structures at work when women who lead an alternative lifestyle frown upon the pairing of certain types of women who are physically attracted to one another, especially because they are all women within a minority community.

Gender Performance: Black Masculinity, White Patriarchy, "the Stud"

I spent a large portion of this chapter discussing Black masculinity and Black manhood as it relates to Black men as they perceive their masculinity and the sociohistorical factors that contribute to Black male identity—a masculine identity that is also reinforced by the gangsta rapper archetype. Black men as tough, savage, aloof, and dominant has been and continues to be perpetuated in the media and within Black culture as a whole. The Black male image is a commodity. The Black lesbian community is not immune to the symptoms of White patriarchy. Black manhood needs to be redefined and challenged and one can argue that President Barrack Obama, as the first Black president, portrays a new archetype of Black masculinity, challenging hegemonic masculinity and creating a new way of imagining Black men. However, within the lesbian community we see studs or butch women emulating a Black hegemonic masculinity. Not only does the stud-femme dichotomy reproduce and produce heteronormativity within lesbian relationships, it also raises questions of self-rejection and the privileging of masculinity. The phenomena of studs rejecting their femaleness and maintaining their dominance (see Wilson, 2009) through gender presentation (not all studs do this) and sexual prowess can be evidence of the stud's discomfort or rejection of her biological body parts. This dominance and sexual prowess dynamic is a well-documented phenomena in the Black lesbian community and, as such, the Black Queer Identity Matrix as discussed in this chapter posits that Black lesbian women, often adopt these communication styles (for example, gender presentation styles, etc.) and practices as they navigate and learn to survive within a dominant and oppressive system. This is one such example of the adoption of a communication style through gender expression and performance.

Within the lesbian community, studs or tomboys have been known to associate or relate to other studs as if femme- or more feminine-identified women cannot understand or relate to the lesbian stud. The book *Black*

Lesbian in White America (1983), by Anita Cornwell, discusses an incident in which women who identified as studs (a term she expresses she hates in the book) implied that they could not relate or befriend women who are more feminine.

The butch-femme dichotomy persists, in part, due to lesbian women emulating Black men, who suffer from Black hegemonic masculinity, which reinforces the privileging of masculinity in constructing meaning. Thus, "studs" are only reflecting back and performing an image of the Black male subject, which is an image that suffers from a void in imagining anything outside of what a Black man is supposed to be. In the end, it further confirms males' status of privilege, which further oppresses women as well as the Black lesbian community. Black lesbian women emulate a Black masculinity that is, in essence, reflective of an operative myth, which is demonstrative of the identity matrix in which Black lesbian women find themselves. Black men seek to emulate a White patriarchal archetype that has never been designed for them to live up to, and Black studs emulate this identity through rejection of femaleness and reinforcing masculine dominance. In the end, we have a phenomena of the reproduction or redefining of White patriarchy and heterosexual relationships within the lesbian community as well as the privileging of masculinity.

Research that links the communicative experiences of different marginalized groups is important (see Orbe, 1998). As discussed here, the Black Queer Identity Matrix allows one to extrapolate the variables of race, gender, and sexual orientation while considering cultural, social, and historical underpinnings unique to the Black lesbian community.

> Exploring the various ways in which those without societal power devise communication tactics when communicating with those with power is a valuable point of examination for communication researchers. Beyond providing an intersection for scholarly inquiry related to culture, power, and communication, it also represents a celebration of human creativity. Second, analysis of common strategies used by those marginalized by dominant society informs the development of human communication theory. (Orbe, p. 32).

As mentioned above, Black lesbians are members within an environment that has the power to shape one's sense of self and rearrange/challenge one's own worldview. Black lesbian women are a product of all the nuances of the United States that influence one's communication patterns as well as one's own self-awareness–this is the major notion I seek to express here. The analysis of the stud-femme dichotomy, particularly the nuances of the stud personification, demonstrates the ways in which Black lesbian women are products of the complexities of their history and an oppressive society, but it also demonstrates the communication patterns, through gender presentation and performance, that many Black lesbian women have adopted in coping or navigating within society.

Gender expression should remain fluid and un-policed, however the personification/ expression of ones identity (especially an identity which is ubiquitous in ones community) should not go without critical examination (along the lines of cultural, societal, and historical underpinnings) of the ways in which the gender has been constructed in order to extrapolate the often oppressive, mechanisms which lead to such a performance.

Bibliography

Anzaldúa, E. (1991). To(o) queer the writer: Loca, escrita y chicana. In B. Warland (Ed.), *Inversions: Writing by dykes and lesbians* (pp. 249-259). Vancouver: Press Gang.

Asante, M. K. (1988). *Afrocentricity*. Trenton, NJ: Africa World.

Asante, M. K. (1990). *Kemet, Afrocentricity, and knowledge*. Trenton, NJ: Africa World.

Asante, M. (2003). *Afrocentricity: The theory of social practice* (Rev. & exp. ed.). Chicago: African American Images.

Balaji, M. (2009). Owning Black masculinity: The intersection of cultural commodification and self-construction in rap music videos. *Communication, Culture & Critique, 2*(1), 21-38.

Bearman, S., Korobov, N., & Thorne, A. (2009). The fabric of internalized sexism. *Journal of Integrated Social Sciences, 1*(1), 10-47.

Bobo, J. (1995). *Black women as cultural readers*. New York: Columbia University Press.

Bowleg, L. (2008). When Black + Woman + Lesbian? ≠ Black Lesbian Woman: The methodological challenges of qualitative and quantitative intersectionality research. *Sex Roles, 59*(5-6), 312-325.

Boykin, K. (1996). *One more river to cross: Black and gay in America*. New York: Anchor.

Butler, J. (1990). Performative acts and gender constitution: An essay in phenomenology and feminist theory. In Sue-Ellen Case (Ed.), *Performing feminisms: Feminist critical theory and theatre* (pp. 270-282). Baltimore: Johns Hopkins University Press.

Collins, P. H. (1986). Learning from the outsider within: The sociological significance of Black feminist thought. *Social Problems, 33*(6), S14-S32.

Collins, P. (2009). *Black feminist thought: Knowledge, consciousness, and the politics of empowerment*. London: HarperCollins Academic.

Cornwell, A. (1983). *Black lesbian in white America*. Tallahassee, FL: Naiad.

Dougherty, D. (2001). Sexual harassment as [dys]functional process: A feminist standpoint analysis. *Journal of Applied Communication Research, 29*(4), 372-402.

Fredrickson, B., & Roberts, T. (1997). Objectification theory: Toward understanding women's lived experiences and mental health risks. *Psychology of Women Quarterly, 21*, 173-206.

Gutiérrez, K. D., & Rogoff, B. (2003). Cultural ways of learning: Individual traits or repertoires of practice. *Educational researcher, 32*(5), 19-25.

Halberstam, J. (1998). *Female Masculinity*. Durham, NC: Duke University Press.

Harris, S. M. (1995). Psychosocial development and Black male masculinity: Implications for counseling economically disadvantaged African American male adolescents. *Journal of Counseling & Development, 73*(3), 279-287.

Hartsock, P. C. M. (1997). *The feminist standpoint revisited and other essays.* Boulder, CO: Westview.

Hartsock, P. C. M. (1983). *Money, sex, and power: Toward a feminist historical materialism.* New York: Longman.

Hartsock, P. C. M. (1998). *The feminist standpoint revisited and other essays.* Boulder, CO: Westview.

Hill, M. R., & Thomas, V. (2000). Strategies for racial identity development: Narratives of Black and White women in interracial partner relationships. *Family Relations: Interdisciplinary Journal of Applied Family Studies, 49,* 193-200.

Howard, S. C. (2011). An autoethnographic study of the interpersonal experiences of a single, Black, lesbian at an HBCU. In E. Gilchrist (Ed.), *Experiences of single, women professors: With this PhD I thee wed* (pp. 159-174). Lanham, MD: Lexington.

Howard, S. C., & Lewis, M. (2011). African American lesbians watching *The L Word*: Audience research. In T. Morrison (Ed.), *Sexual minority research in the new millennium* (pp 107-126). New York: Nova Science.

Hurt, B. (Dir.). (2006). *Hip-hop: Beyond beats & rhymes.* (DVD). United States: Media Education Foundation.

Jackson, R. L. (2006). *Scripting the Black masculine body: Identity, discourse, and racial politics in popular media.* Albany: State University of New York Press.

Lane-Steele, Laura. "Studs and protest-hypermasculinity: The tomboyism within Black lesbian female masculinity." *Journal of lesbian studies* 15.4 (2011): 480-492.

Majors, R. (1989). Cool pose: The proud signature of Black survival. In M. Kimmel & M. Messner (Eds.), *Men's lives* (pp. 83-86). New York: Macmillan.

Majors, R., & Billson, J. (1992). *Cool pose: The dilemmas of Black manhood in America.* New York: Touchstone.

Mazama, A. (2001). The Afrocentric paradigm: Contours and definitions. *Journal of Black Studies, 31*(4), 387-405.

Messerschmidt, J. (2000). *Nine lives: Adolescent masculinities, the body, and violence.* Boulder, CO: Westview.

Moore, M. R. (2006). Lipstick or Timberlands? Meanings of gender presentation in Black lesbian communities. *Signs, 32*(1), 113-139.

Munoz, J. (1991). *Disidentifications: Queers of color and the performance of politics.* Minneapolis: University of Minnesota Press.

Neal, M. (2006). *New black man.* New York: Routledge.

Nichols, J. (2006). *The realest nigga: Constructions of Black masculinity within rap music.* University of Maryland, College Park. ProQuest Dissertations and Theses, p. 66. Retrieved from http://search.proquest.com/docview/305306294?accountid=2909

Nielsen, l. M. (Ed.). (1990). *Feminist research methods: Exemplary readings in the social sciences.* Boulder, CO: Westview Press.

Orbe, M. P. (1998). *Constructing co-cultural theory: An explication of culture, power, and communication.* Thousand Oaks, CA: Sage.

Oware. (2010). Brotherly love: Homosociality and Black masculinity in Gangdta Rao music. *Journal of African American Studies, 15*, 22-39.

Pemberton, J. M. (2008). *"Now I ain't sayin' she's a gold digger": African American femininities in rap music lyrics.* Florida State University. ProQuest Dissertations and Theses, p. 224. Retrieved from http://search.proquest.com/docview/89272038?accountid=2909

Roberts-Douglass, K., & Curtis-Boles, H. (2012). Exploring positive masculinity development in African American men: A retrospective study. *Psychology of Men & Masculinity, 14*(1), 7-15.

Ross, M. B. (1998). In search of black men's masculinities. *Feminist Studies, 24*(3), 599-626.

Rubin, G. (1992). Of catamites and kings: Reflections on butch, gender, and boundaries. In J. Nestle (Ed.), *The persistent desire. a femme-butch-reader* (pp. 466-482). Boston: Alyson.

Rux, C. H. (2003). Eminem: The new White Negro. In Greg Tate (Ed.), *Everything but the burden* (pp. 15-38). New York: Broadway.

Smith, D. E. (1987). *The everyday world as problematic.* Boston: Northeastern University Press.

Stanback, M. H., & Pearce, W. B. (1981). Talking to "the man": Some communication strategies used by members of "subordinate" social groups. *Quarterly Journal of Speech, 67*(1), 21-30.

Swigonski, Mary E. (1994). "The logic of feminist standpoint theory for social work research." *Social Work, 39*(4), 387-393.

Swim, J. K., & Hyers, L. L. (1999). Excuse me—What did you just say?!: Women's public and private responses to sexist remarks. *Journal of Experimental Social Psychology, 35*(1), 68-88.

Taylor, V., & Rupp, L. (1993). Women's culture and lesbian feminist activism: A reconsideration of cultural feminism. *Signs, 19*, 32-61.

Tolman, D. L., & Porche, M. V. (2000). The Adolescent Femininity Ideology Scale: Development and validation of a new measure for girls. *Psychology of Women Quarterly, 24*(4), 365-376.

West, R., & Turner, L. H. (2010). *Introduction to communication theory: Analysis and application* (3rd ed.). Boston: McGraw-Hill.

Wilson, B. (2009). Black lesbian gender and sexual culture: Celebration and resistance. *Culture, Health and Sexuality, 3*, 297-313.

Epilogue

This volume has been a culmination of academic work and personal association as it relates to Black lesbian female identity. I spent much of this book presenting a need for a more integrated queer of color framework. Hopefully, the Black Queer Identity Matrix (BQIM) will be a starting place for discussion and scholarship around Black lesbian women.

I believe Afrocentricity gives us the foundation to comprehend the continuity and extension between African American history and communication within the Black community today. Black women are members of the Black community and consequently have a very unique cultural history, which is significant in studying members of the Black community. Molefi Asante is considered "the father" of Afrocentricity and began his work in the field of rhetoric. This is significant in that the foundation of Afrocentricity encourages us to explore the communicative or rhetorical dimensions within African American communication. Afrocentricity provides a vehicle to exploring these communicative strategies that may be unique to African American women. There is a large body of knowledge around Black Rhetoric and Black Liberation Rhetoric, with very little focus on women. BQIM seeks to explore these communicative associations across the African American lesbian community. It is not to say that all African American women employ the same communication strategies when negotiating their identity, coming out, or coping with oppression within society; however, I am saying that Black women have a unique history that influences how they communicate, how their worldview is shaped, and how they view themselves. Being a minority on three counts forces one to be equipped with strategies to cope with the racism, sexism, and heterosexism that will certainly take place in one's life. Likewise, standpoint theory provides an important foundation to the comprehension and examination of the Black lesbian woman. Assumptions of standpoint theory allow for the BQIM to examine the dynamics of power and the importance of gaining vital knowledge from everyday people. BQIM is less about attempting to argue that Black woman have a more accurate view of oppression and hierarchy and more about attempting to position everyday Black lesbian women as the individuals who hold vital knowledge about their lived experiences. The BQIM seeks to focus research, which creates an outlet for women to be heard through qualitative, ethnographic inquiry. Guided by standpoint theory, BQIM rests on the assumption that different social locations and social knowledge' often produce distinct communication patterns.

For BQIM, inclusion of Patricia Hill Collins's matrix of domination as a starting place for theorizing rests on the understanding that Black lesbian female identity should be studied and understood from an intersectional approach. Although, at times, it may be methodologically challenging to conduct research projects that do not treat one's identity as additive, as opposed to intersectional, BQIM challenges researchers to steer away from language that encourages Black lesbian women to rank their identities. It has been a challenge within this text to consistently view analysis through an intersectional lens; however, it is an important challenge to overcome. For individuals who are minorities on three counts, there is no hierarchy of oppression as it relates to race, gender, and sexual orientation. They all work together as interlocking systems of oppression to create unique experiences, understandings, and worldviews.

The utilization of a framework such as BQIM encourages the explication and examination of historical, cultural, and social underpinnings within and across the African American community as race has largely been ignored in queer theory scholarship.

Personal Reflections

As a Black lesbian working in academe I realize I speak from a privileged position. Much of my time is spent working with an "elite" group of people in academe, who are often charged with being out of touch or creating work that is only read by a small group of people. The intention of this volume is not only to speak to a small group of people in academe but also to reach those outside of academe. Those who fall into different social classes, work in different fields, and live in different regions across the country have a wide variety of experiences, outside of my day-to-day experiences, and BQIM seeks to bring various experiences, reflections, and standpoints within the Black lesbian community to the forefront. I strongly believe that even with the varied demographics of lesbian women of color, there are still common struggles, a common history, and common experiences that create a special bond, a special understanding, and special relationships. These common experiences need to be illuminated, as recognizing and ultimately accepting difference is key to coexistence. Perhaps these common struggles and experiences around race, gender, and sexual orientation can be further explored and expanded upon as researchers create frameworks allowing us to effectively analyze these variables.

As a researcher positing a conceptual framework that seeks to explore relationships and connections among race, gender, and sexual orientation, it is imperative that I am self-reflexive and conscious of the ways in which my identities work together as interlocking systems of oppression as well as privilege. Applying the assumptions of BQIM to my social identities through an autoethnographic approach is valuable in creating a more clear vision of BQIM and of myself. In our day-to-day lives, it is not often that one can reflect on one's social identities and the history of those identities through examination of how they work together. This epilogue will conclude with an autoethnographic evaluation of myself.

Autoethnography is defined as an "autobiographical genre of writing and research that displays multiple layers of consciousness, connecting the personal to the cultural" (Ellis & Bochner, 2000, p. 739). Autoethnography is a form of self-authorship that moves an individual from merely external constructions to more complex internal ones. According to Baxter Magolda (2001), self-authorship is captured by "the driving questions of how do I know? who am I? how do I construct relationships with others?" (p. 15). BQIM encourages this connection of the personal to the cultural.

I am a woman, a lesbian, a sister, a daughter, a friend, a professor, and so many other identities that tie me to the culture of a particular group. As I reflect on my social identities I think about my personal relationships with friends and family. It took me several years to disclose my sexual orientation to my family and to certain friends who I thought would not be accepting of it. Eventually, I was able to overcome my fear and become the person I am today. My grandmother has always been very religious and I always knew she would be the hardest person to disclose to. The element of religion has always frightened me in relation to sexual orientation. The friends that I have, and have had, who are very religious have always been the last ones to know my sexual orientation. To me, Christianity (which most of my friends and family members are) and sexual orientation are not reconcilable; I cannot understand how one can adhere to Christianity and be accepting of the LGBTQ community because of what I have read in the Bible and how many members of the religious right interpret sexual orientation in the Bible. I have friends who are religious and who are on the LGBTQ spectrum and I am constantly trying to understand how they reconcile the two. I realize that the Black community has a long connection to the Black church, as the Black church was a major place of solidarity and strength during the civil rights movement. I also realize that the Bible and faith were the major sources of strength pre- and post-Civil War, so it is not surprising to me that the Black community struggles with homophobia—all things must be understood and viewed through the continuity of historical and cultural underpinnings. The friends and family that I do have stand strong in their belief system but also accept me for the person that I am, regardless of my sexual orientation.

For individuals like myself who have to "come out" in order to live a happy, healthy life, there are several factors that make the transition fearful. The fact of the matter is one really never knows how family or friends will react when one does come out. I always viewed my immediate family to be open and nonjudgmental, but I stilled questioned how open and nonjudgmental they would be with something so close to home—it is different when it is one's daughter, or son, or sister, or brother. Coming out is hard because you just never know. There are countless amounts of LGBTQ people who have been put out of the house, abandoned, fired, and killed because of their sexual orientation. As much as some people argue that members of the LGBTQ community do not experience a minority status or discrimination, the fact of the matter is there is discrimination against members of the LGBTQ community. I have been denied access to places because of my gender expression, I have been kicked out of a diner for kissing another woman on the lips, and I have been told I was going to hell by people I considered friends. These things may not have taken my life but they do act to rearrange one's worldview and alter one's self-concept, which are essential to mental health. For me these instances served to reinforce heteronormativity and make it clear that coming out or being authentically me was not going to be easy. Ultimately, my negative experiences have served to make me a stronger, better person. These experiences are not over and coming out is a lifelong process as every new space I enter introduces a new space to negotiate my sexual identity. Every time someone assumes I am a heterosexual I have to negotiate how I will communicate my sexual orientation or even if I will communicate my sexual orientation. I do not always feel safe doing so.

As a graduate student I did not feel safe disclosing my sexual orientation. As I think back, my primary concern with disclosing my sexual orientation was the fact that I attended a historically Black college-university (HBCU). HBCU's are institutions that usually adhere to strong Christian values. Therefore, homophobia was a major concern for me, as strong Christian values and a lesbian identity usually do not co-exist. I also had no one to remain in solidarity with that was immediately accessible to me. Meaning, I did not know any other Black lesbian women in my program of study to confide in or come out with! The importance of community connectedness and a strong support system was never more evident to me than during the time of my graduate studies. I never felt like I had a support system during that time. I was my own support system. I came out alone, I dealt with discrimination alone, and I overcame my fears alone. Ultimately, the choice and the courage to come out is a solitary decision and process. You may have people in your life that support you but you are out in the world alone, you deal with the consequences alone. Thinking back on my coming-out process and this acceptance of self, I see very clearly the identity matrix I speak of in this text. My coming-out process during graduate school was layered with fears of the HBCU institution. Being my authentic self was connected to the values of the social system of the HBCU in which I was a part of. I did not want to be subject to heterosexist values and language within the institution, within the department in which I studied. Thus, my fears were socially constructed due to the structure in which I was a part of. The structure ultimately made me who I am today. The structure of the institution ultimately made me stronger—it could have easily went a different way. On a more macro-level, the region that I was living in—Washington, D.C.—also constructed how I dressed and how I perceived myself. To me, Washington, D.C., was very accepting of my sexual orientation and greatly influenced my gender expression. Had I lived somewhere else, I may not have expressed my gender in the ways in which I did. For example, I went through a phase of dressing more along the lines of a tomboy or masculine because I felt comfortable doing that in the area in which I lived. When I would go to and from school, however, I did not feel comfortable dressing in that manner. All of these things constructed my identity and arranged my worldview on how I identified, how I negotiated my sexual orientation, how I expressed my gender.

I realize now that my sexual orientation is a social construct. For me, this means identifying as a lesbian is essentially a label that has been created for me to fit into. This does not take away from the fact that I am sexually attracted to women and not men. However, categories such as lesbian, gay, bisexual, and others are essentially approximations of reality. Not everyone perfectly or neatly fits into those categories—which is why they keep adding letters to the acronym LGBTQ. Categories never quite get it right. For example, someone will call themselves "lesbian" if their experiences have involved only same-sex attraction and behavior because that's who they're principally attracted to, but that doesn't necessarily mean that they'll never be involved with a member of the opposite sex or at least find a member of the opposite sex attractive or sexually attractive. Ultimately, I believe if social expectations and enforcements were removed, people would grow however they felt best fit them. In other words, people wouldn't feel the need to conform to "Blackness" or a "lesbian" identity, and so on—they would simply be. Labels tend to limit possibilities of what one can or does become.

As a professor, I realize I am a part of a privileged class of working people but, even being a part of this privileged class, I still feel and see patterns of racial, sexual-oriented, and gendered microaggressions. I am not going to go into the intricacies of these microaggressions here; however, struggle remains a centerpiece within my existence. As a young Black lesbian professor I do feel as though I am treated differently and respected differently than my counterparts, and, of course, this is through the subjective lens of a my social identities. This treatment does, however, create distinct and often conscious communication patterns as I navigate throughout the university. The BQIM is a conceptual framework that seeks to further explicate the nuances of various variables within and across the Black lesbian community, including those that consider themselves bisexual, questioning, working class, blue collar, white collar, and so on.

The BQIM is not only for discussion around the intersections of race, gender, and sexual orientation but also to allow for discussion around the multiplicity of identities within and across the Black lesbian community. For example, I am Black, a lesbian, a daughter, a sister, a professor, and the list goes on, which provide me with an array of experiences that arrange and rearrange my worldview. This is true for all of the Black lesbian community. All of these identities create unique experiences and allow us, at times, to access realms of privilege as well as oppression. The BQIM seeks to explore these identities, while acknowledging the reality of race, gender, and sexual orientation as identities that have been historically oppressed. BQIM is to study what we have in common but also how we are different. The BQIM also leaves room to dis-identify with identities, by exploring the ways in which self-identified Black lesbian women dis-identify with Blackness or lesbianism or with womanism, or to live outside the notions of what *Black* is or what being a *lesbian* is. What are the possibilities and realms of experience within the identity matrix?

Notes

"Queer," in this volume, is used to denote an individual who does not self-identify as heterosexual or any individual who challenges the binary of what is considered traditionally masculine or feminine.

"Woman" and "female" are used interchangeably (though there are compelling arguments to isolate the two) to identify an organism of the sex or sexual phase that normally produces egg cells.

I use "Black" and "African American" throughout this text, though there are certainly compelling arguments to isolate the two; Black or African American refers to peoples throughout the diaspora who live in the United States and are of African descent. These individuals share common histories and positionalities and overall struggle discussed throughout this volume.

Bibliography

Baxter Magolda, M. (2001). *Making their own way: Narratives for transforming higher education to promote self-development*. Sterling, VA: Stylus.

Ellis, C., & Bochner, A. (2000). Autoethnography, personal narrative, reflexivity. In Norman K. Denzin & Yvonna S. Lincoln (Eds.), *Handbook of qualitative research* (2nd ed., pp. 733-768). Thousand Oaks, CA: Sage.

Index

-A-

A Burst of Light: Essays, 2
African American Lesbians Watching The L Word, 6
Afrocentricity, 65, 66, 69-73, 95
Alimahomed, S., 2
American Journal of Public Health, 54
Amherst College, 30
Ang, I., 43
Anzaldúa, G., 19, 20
Asante, M., 65, 69, 70, 71, 73, 95
autoethnography, xv, 97

-B-

Balaji, M., 84
Barrett, D.C., 11
Barthes, R., 41
Baucham, V., 25
Bearman, S., 87, 88
Billson, J., 72, 80, 81
Black diasporic cultural community, 82
Black feminism, 31-34, 34-35
Black Feminist Thought, 4, 31, 72
Black hegemonic masculinity, 77, 89, 90
Black lesbian female community
   communication strategies, 61
   health disparities in, 53-54
   homophobia about, 70
   photographic representations of, 49-51
   religion and, 54, 97
   study of, 45-49
   White patriarchy and, 89
Black lesbian female identity, xv
   Black hegemonic masculinity and, 89

butch-femme dichotomy, 29-30, 77-79, 84-89
   coexistence and, 57-59
   intersectionality and, 1-3
Black Lesbian in White America, 90
Black lesbians, vii, viii, xiii
   empirical literature about, 40
   empowerment and, 55-57
   feminist movement and, 30
   intersectionality and, 1-3
   invisibility of, 39-40, 42
   media representations of, 6, 42-43, 51, 60
   racial issues and, 31
   religion and, 54-55
   three oppressed identities of, 40, 43, 52, 61, 66, 87, 90, 95
Black Liberation Rhetoric, 95
Black males
   functional myth of, 80
   hip-hop culture, 81, 83, 84
   rebel image of, 83
   rap music, 81
Black masculinity, 79-84, 89-91
Black Queer Identity Matrix, xv, 3, 4, 25, 29, 51-55, 60, 67, 95-97
   Afrocentricity and, 70
   Black gender expression and, 76-79
   critique of, 76
   definition, xvi
   heteronormativity,
   implications of, 73-74
   integral assumptions about, 74-75
   intersectionality and, 1-3, 39
   overview of, 39-40
   photo feedback and, 39, 45
   standpoint theory and, 39, 95

theoretical framework of, 65–67
Black Rhetoric, 95
Black women
  Afrocentricity and, 95
  feminism and, 32
  representation, 42–43
  White women and, 33–34
  women's rights movement and, 31–32
Bobo, J., 42, 43, 44, 74
Bochner, A., 97
Bowleg, L., 2, 3, 9, 40, 44, 55, 66, 74
Boykin, K., 72
Brah, A., 44
Braun, V., 48
Burris, M., 45, 46
butch-femme dichotomy, 29–30, 77–79, 84–89
Butkin, J., 7
Butler, J., 16, 17, 83

-C-

Cade, T., 33
Calderone, L., 31
Californina Marriage Protection Act, 22
Cannick, J., 23
Cartwright, L., 41, 42
Centers for Disease Control, 7, 8
Champeau, D.A., 5, 7, 8
Charoula, 31
Chuck D, 83
civil rights movement, 25–27, 97–98
Clarke, V., 48
Close, H., 46
Coalition of African American Pastors, 26
Cochran, S.D., 39, 40
Cohen, C.J., 16
Coleman, A., 26
Collier, J., 46
Collier, M., 45
Collins, P.H., xiv, 2, 3, 4, 5, 31, 32, 33, 35, 44, 65, 67, 72, 73, 74, 80, 96
Combahee River Collective, 2, 33
Committee for the Survival of a Free Congress, 26
community connectedness, 11

Conerly, G., 71
Connors, M., 8
connotative meaning, 41
Constructing Co-cultural Theory, 75
coolness, 80
Cornwell, A., 90
Crenshaw, K., 2, 9
critical race studies, 16
Crocker, J., 11
Curtis-Boles, H., 79, 80

-D-

Deconstruction, 16
DeGeneres, E., 6
de Lauretis, T., 16, 18
denotative meaning, 41
Derrida, J., 16
difference, theory of, 58
domination, matrix of, 3–4, 5–7, 7–11, 65, 66, 72, 73, 96
Dougherty, D., 69

-E-

Ellis, C., 97
Epistemology of the Closet, The, 17
Eschholz, S., 7
essentialism, 44
ethnography, xv

-F-

feminism, 31, 33
feminist studies, 16
femme-on-femme relationships, 87
femmes, 77, 78
Ferguson, R., 2
Foucault, M., 16
Frederickson, B., 88
Frost, D.M., 10

-G-

gangsta rap, 89
Garber, E., 31
gay and lesbian studies, 16
gay marriage, 22-24
gay rights movement, 22-24
    civil rights movement and, 25-27
    White privilege and, 27-29
gender, 17, 72-73
Glascock, J., 7
GLBTQ, 29
Glunt, E.K., 11
Grace Family Baptist Church, 25
Gutiérrez, K.D., 88

-H-

Halferty, J., vii
Halperin, D.M., 16, 18
Hariman, R., 41
Harper, D., 48
Hartsock, N.C.M., 43-44, 65, 67, 68, 73
Hatzenbuehler, M.L., 10
healthcare, 7-11
Hearth and Home, 7
hegemonic masculinity, 82
Herek, G.M., 11
heterosexuality, viii
Hill, M.R., 87
Hip-Hop: Beyond Beats and Rhymes, 82
hip-hop culture, 81-84
HIV/AIDS, 5, 7, 8, 9
hooks, B., 2, 4
Howard, S.C., 6, 39, 42, 43, 48, 66, 74
Hull, G.T., 2
Hurt, B., 82
Hyers, L.L., 87
hypermasculinity, 80, 82

-I-

identity, 5
In Search of Our Mothers' Gardens, 32

intersectionality, 1, 8-11, 19, 39, 44-45, 59-60

-J-

Jackson, R.L., 72
Jagose, A., 18, 19
Johnson, E.P., 15, 19, 20, 21
Jordan, J., 33

-K-

Keats, J., 47
Kemet, Afrocentricity, and Knowledge, 71
Keyes, K.M., 10
Klein, H., 7
Korobov, N., 87, 88

-L-

L Word, The, 6, 42
Lane-Steele, L., 77, 79, 84
language, power of, 16
Lee, W., 20
lesbianism, 34
Lewis, M., 6, 39, 42, 43, 48, 66
LGBTQ community, viii
    Black religious leaders and, 26
    civil rights movement and, 25-26
    communication strategies, 61
    connectedness and, 11
    health disparities in, 54
    HIV/AIDS and, 9
    mainstream media and, 6
    poverty and, 28
    race relations and, 21-22
    racism and, 29
    White privilege and, 28-29
Lincoln, C.E., 54
Long, J., 7
Lorde, A., xiv, 2, 30, 33, 34, 35, 58, 85
Los Angeles Times, The, 22
Lucaites, J., 41

-M-

Mack-Nataf, I., vii
Magolda, B., 97
Major, B., 11
Majors, R., 72, 80, 81
Mamiya, L.H., 54
Marinak, B., 47
masculinity, 72
matrix, xvi, 76
matrix of domination, 3-4, 5-7, 7-11, 65, 66, 72, 73, 96
Mays, V.M., 39, 40
Mazama, A., 71
McCall, L., 45
McLaughlin, K.A., 10
Meyer, I.H., 10, 11
Moore, M.R., 30, 31, 50, 52, 60, 78, 84, 85
Moraga, C., 19
Morland, I., 19
Mũnoz, 21
Murray, S.O., 29

-N-

Namaste, K., 16
National Communication Association, 29
National Library of Medicine, 54
Neal, M., 80
Nichols, J., 84
Nielson, I.M., 67

-O-

Obama, B., 22, 23, 24, 89
O'Brien, L.T., 11
Orbe, M.P., 67, 75, 90
O'Reilly, B., 24
others, 57
Oware, 80
Owens, W., 25

-P-

Pearce, W.B., 75
Pemberton, J.M., 81
performative reflexivity, 21
performativity, 84
Phan, K.T., 36
Phillips, D., 42, 43
Phoenix, A., 44
photo feedback analysis, 47
photovoice, 45, 46
Pies, C.A., 46
Pink, S., 46
Poem, xiv
politics of domination, 4
Pollack, L.M., 11
Porsche, M.V., 88
positivism, 41
postmodernism, 16
postracial America, 27
Preston-Schreck, C., 7
Professor Griff, 83
Proposition 8, 22, 23, 24, 27
Public Enemy, 83

-Q-

Quare Theory, 15, 19-21
queer, vii, 15
queer studies, vii, 65, 71
queer theory, viii, 15-19

-R-

race, 25, 72-73
Race Matters, 5
race relations, 21-22
rap music, 81
Responses to Discrimination and Psychiatric Disorders and Black, Hispanic, Female, and Lesbian, Gay, and Bisexual Individuals, 10
Richie, B., 34
Roberts, T., 88
Roberts-Douglass, K., 79, 80

Rofes, E.E., 28
Rogoff, B., 88
Rose, T., 83
Ross, M.B., 82
Rubin, G., 85
RuPaul, 21
Rupp, L., 85
Rux, C.H., 82

-S-

Sampson-Cordle, A., 46
Samuels, J., 48
Sapinoso, J.V., 20
Savage, D., 23
Scott, P.B., 2
Sedgwick, E.K., 16, 17, 18
sexism, 88
sexual orientation, 72-73
shared emotional connection, 10
Shaw, S.M., 5, 7, 8
Shiffman, K.S., 7
Sister Outsider, 30
Smith, B., xiv, 2, 30, 34
Smith, D.E., 67
Smyth, C., vii
social justice, 33
social location, 5
Stanback, M.H., 75
standpoint theory, 39, 43-44, 49, 57, 59, 65, 66, 73, 95, 96
  five assumptions of, 68-69
  fundamental tenets of, 67-69
  Marxism and, 69
Stephens, D., 42, 43
Stewart, J., 24
Stone, A.L., 22, 24, 25
Strickland, M., 47
stud-femme dichotomy. *See* butch-femme dichotomy
stud-on-stud relationships, 87, 88
studs, 77, 78, 79, 86
Sturken, M., 41, 42
Sullivan, A., 23
supplementarity, 17
Swignoski, M.E., 67

Swim, J.K., 87
symbolic annihilation, 7

-T-

Tally, J., 33
Taylor, V., 85
Teunis, N., 28
Thomas, V., 87
Thorne, A., 87, 88
Tolman, D.L., 88
Tuchman, G., 7
Turner, L.H., 39, 43, 44, 51, 57, 59, 61, 66, 67, 68, 69, 74

-W-

Walker, A., 31, 32
Wang, C., 45, 46
Ward, E.G., 54
Ward, J., 23, 24, 25
Warner, L.R., 44
Warner, M., 16, 17
West, C., 5, 6
West, R., 39, 43, 44, 51, 57, 59, 61, 66, 67, 68, 69, 74
Weyrich, P.M., 26
White privilege/patriarchy, 19, 27-29, 77, 89
White women, 33-34
Whitlock, R., vii
Wilson, B., 84, 85, 86, 87
womanish, 32
womanism, 31-34, 35
womanist, 33
women's rights movement, 29-31
women's studies, 45
Wood, J.T., 44, 49

-Z-

Zami, A New Spelling of My Name, 2

Rochelle Brock &
Richard Greggory Johnson III,
Executive Editors

Black Studies and Critical Thinking is an interdisciplinary series which examines the intellectual traditions of and cultural contributions made by people of African descent throughout the world. Whether it is in literature, art, music, science, or academics, these contributions are vast and far-reaching. As we work to stretch the boundaries of knowledge and understanding of issues critical to the Black experience, this series offers a unique opportunity to study the social, economic, and political forces that have shaped the historic experience of Black America, and that continue to determine our future. Black Studies and Critical Thinking is positioned at the forefront of research on the Black experience, and is the source for dynamic, innovative, and creative exploration of the most vital issues facing African Americans. The series invites contributions from all disciplines but is specially suited for cultural studies, anthropology, history, sociology, literature, art, and music.

Subjects of interest include (but are not limited to):

- Education
- Sociology
- History
- Media/Communication
- Religion/Theology
- Women's Studies

- Policy Studies
- Advertising
- African American Studies
- Political Science
- LGBT Studies

For additional information about this series or for the submission of manuscripts, please contact Dr. Brock (Indiana University Northwest) at brock2@iun.edu or Dr. Johnson (University of San Francisco) at rgjohnsoniii@usfca.edu.

To order other books in this series, please contact our Customer Service Department:

(800) 770-LANG (within the U.S.)
(212) 647-7706 (outside the U.S.)
(212) 647-7707 FAX

Or browse online by series at www.peterlang.com.